Growing Up with Two Languages

The lives of many families involve contact with more than one language and culture on a daily basis. *Growing Up with Two Languages* is aimed at the many parents and professionals who feel uncertain about the best way to go about helping children gain maximum benefit from the situation.

Every family's situation is different, but there is a good deal that parents can do to make life with two languages easier for their children.

This best-selling guide is illustrated by glimpses of life from interviews with fifty families from all around the world. The trials and rewards of life with two languages and cultures are discussed in detail, and followed by practical advice on how to support the child's linguistic development.

Features of this second edition include:

- new and updated Internet resources
- information on the specific problems facing teenagers, and guidance on how to resolve them
- new research into language acquisition
- new and updated first-hand advice and examples throughout.

Una Cunningham-Andersson is a Senior Lecturer in English language and linguistics at Dalarna University in Falun, Sweden. **Staffan Andersson** teaches computing. They are raising their four children to speak English and Swedish in Sweden.

Growing Up with Two Languages

A Practical Guide

Second Edition

Una Cunningham-Andersson
and Staffan Andersson

 Routledge
Taylor & Francis Group

LONDON AND NEW YORK

First published 1999 by Routledge
11 New Fetter Lane, London EC4P 4EE

Reprinted 2000, 2001, 2002 (twice)

Second edition first published 2004 by Routledge
11 New Fetter Lane, London EC4P 4EE

Simultaneously published in the USA and Canada
by Routledge
29 West 35th Street, New York, NY 10001

Routledge is an imprint of the Taylor & Francis Group

© 1999, 2004 Una Cunningham-Andersson and Staffan Andersson

Typeset in Bembo by MHL Typesetting Limited, Coventry, Warwickshire
Printed and bound in Great Britain by T J International Ltd, Padstow, Cornwall

British Library Cataloguing in Publication Data
A catalogue record for this book is available from the British Library

Library of Congress Cataloging in Publication Data
A catalog record for this title has been requested

ISBN 0-415-33331-8 (hbk)
ISBN 0-415-33332-6 (pbk)

For Leif, Anders, Patrik and Elisabeth, who taught us what we know about children

Contents

Preface

For those like ourselves, who grew up using a single language except during foreign language lessons at school, it is a new experience to live great chunks of life through the medium of another language and culture. Even if the second language involved is one that was learned at school, its daily use involves new challenges and rewards. All sorts of issues must be addressed depending on the circumstances, such as the choice of language to be spoken to which people in which situation, and how those involved will acquire reasonable facility in their second language, and what relationship they will have to the non-native culture.

This book is intended for parents who find their everyday life involves two or more languages. The readers we have in mind are not generally part of an established bilingual community in a country, but rather individuals or families who have uprooted and resettled in another linguistic environment, or their partners or children. This raises fascinating issues, such as the question of what it is not to be a native speaker of a language, with full access to the associated culture, and how best to hold your own as a non-native. We will not try to tell you how best to learn a second language, but rather what the effects of dealing with two languages may be for you or your children. There are so many of us in the same boat. Let us learn from each other!

This book is the second edition of a book originally published in 1999. The parts of the text that refer to our own children have been updated, and the sections relating to older children and teenagers have been extended to reflect our experiences. The appendix dealing with Internet resources has, of course, been thoroughly revamped. In the years that have passed since the first edition was published the main thing that has changed is that our children have grown older. Leif is now 17, Anders is 15, Pat is 11 and Lisa is 10. This means that we are better able to see how things have worked out. And we have to say that the long-term results of our own venture with two languages have turned out better than we dared to hope. Two of our four children, Anders and Lisa, are now native-like in both their languages and the other two are very competent in English, but native-like in Swedish only.

We avoid the use of the word *bilingual* to describe people in this book. A person can have a bilingual upbringing, or childhood, and a family can be bilingual or have a bilingual home. That means that two languages are involved. To talk about individuals as bilinguals is difficult. What are the criteria for describing people as bilingual? Would they have to speak their two languages equally well? Would they have to be monolingual-like in both languages? If not, just how much of the weaker language do they need to know to be called bilingual? Is a newborn baby bilingual if the parents speak different languages? Is a pre-school child bilingual if he has passive knowledge of a second language? Is a schoolchild bilingual if she can carry on a conversation in a foreign language? Can an adult raised with one language later become bilingual? Without any degree of consensus as to what the word actually means, its use is not meaningful. For this reason, we prefer the more neutral expression, to live with two languages.

We, the authors, have between us had to face all of these questions. Una is an immigrant to Sweden (she was brought up in Northern Ireland), a foreign language learner (having studied Irish, French and Spanish at school), a second language learner (she lived in Spain for a year and first came into contact with the Swedish language in 1980, at the age of 20) and a parent of four children who are supposed to be growing up with two languages and cultures. Staffan is married to an immigrant (Una) and uses a language which he does not fully master (English) to communicate with his wife. He is also a parent of (the same) four children who are living with English and Swedish.

We have often felt the need for some kind of manual to consult. Just as we have a family medical book and a child development book, we would like to be able to look up the answers to our questions concerning life with two languages and cultures. There are excellent books which help parents and teachers deal with children with two languages, such as those by George Saunders (1982), Lenore Arnberg (1987) and Colin Baker (1995), but we have found nothing to answer questions about the wider issue of how adults and children are affected by living with two languages and cultures, and how language and culture are related to each other in such a situation. We hope that this book may fill that gap.

For anyone who is curious about our story, we met on 16 July 1980 on a train in Niš, in what was then Yugoslavia, when Staffan was travelling from Uppsala to the Black Sea and Una from Nottingham to Israel. Neither of us reached our destinations! We now live with our children in the depths of the Swedish forests, near Uppsala.

If you would like to contribute your own experiences for possible inclusion in a future edition of this book, or comment on any part of this book, please do not hesitate to get in touch with us.

Una Cunningham-Andersson and Staffan Andersson
(liljansberg@swipnet.se)
Liljansberg, Sweden

Acknowledgements

We have gathered personal accounts of life with two languages from some 150 individuals and families in the Internet community. They have generously shared their experiences of what has worked well or not so well when living with two languages within the family. We can learn a lot from the experiences of others who have faced the same issues as we do now and have had to deal with them. Thank you all of you who have given us a glimpse of your lives with two or more languages.

Chapter 1

Families with two languages

Background

There have always been those who have moved from one country to another to study or work for a while. The expansion of the European Union (EU) has led to ever-increasing numbers of Europeans who move from one country to another within Europe. In addition, many people have come to the countries of Western Europe as refugees from conflicts in other parts of the world or in what was once Yugoslavia. In Japan, Korea and Taiwan, as well as parts of the Middle East, Africa and South America, there are many foreign workers, often married to local people. USA, Canada and Australia have, by their very nature, large immigrant populations. People are living abroad all over the world for innumerable reasons.

The reasons behind a move from one country to another have a lot to do with how the move will turn out. If a family goes to live in another country because one or both of the parents have got a job there, the situation is quite dissimilar to when a single person moves from one country to another to make a family with a native of the new country. Both these situations are radically different from that faced by refugee families who flee from a war zone to take refuge in a peaceful country. All of these immigrants have some things in common. They are all faced with learning the language and becoming familiar with the culture of their new country, but they probably have very contrasting expectations of how well they will succeed at these tasks and how long they are likely to stay in the new country. They are, therefore, not equally motivated to throw themselves into their new situations.

Mixed language families and intercultural marriage

Some adults who become involved with two languages are in the position that they have met and fallen in love with a person who has a different first language from themselves. Two languages generally mean two cultures, although a couple can have separate cultures without speaking different languages. Examples of this are an American–British couple or a Mozambique–Portuguese couple, or even a couple where one comes from, say, northern Italy and the other from Sicily. This kind of relationship is fraught with potential misunderstandings and unspoken expectations and assumptions which need to be made explicit given the couple's lack of a common background.

Language choice

A family with two languages will usually find a regular way of defining how the languages are used, depending on where they live and how well the parents each speak the other's language. A French–German couple living in Germany may thus speak French between themselves and German in the company of others. If, however, they started out using one or other language together, perhaps because one of them did not then speak the other's language, they may not be able to change easily if there comes a time when it would make more sense to speak the other language. When children come along, they will need to be accommodated in the couple's linguistic arrangements.

Example

An American woman and a Swedish man met while they were both studying in Germany. They began by speaking German together. When they subsequently married and moved to Sweden they gradually started to speak English together. When the woman started learning Swedish she wanted them to speak Swedish together, which they still do although it is alternated with English, depending on the subject matter. When their son was born, they each spoke their own native language with him.

Our own story is that Una (from Northern Ireland) met Staffan (from Sweden) travelling in Eastern Europe. We had no choice but to speak English, our only common language. Later, when Una moved to Sweden and learned Swedish, we continued to speak English together, because of our mutual reluctance to speak Swedish to each other, even when Una's knowledge of Swedish became greater than Staffan's knowledge of English. We each speak our own language with our children.

However the mixed language couple decide to organise their linguistic system, one or both of them will at any given time be using a language other than their own to communicate. The partner will be left with the task of talking and listening to a person who probably does not have a full mastery of the language being used. The couple will, of course, become very used to this set-up, and no longer really hear any foreign accent or faulty grammar that the other may have. Their children, however, may delight in correcting their parents' non-native errors in each language, if they do not find them embarrassing.

To a certain extent, the non-native speaker will learn from the native speaker, but for most couples, linguistic correctness cannot be allowed to stand in the way of communication. Not many people want to think about the correct form to be used when they are planning what to buy for supper, still less do they want to be corrected by their partner. The learning that does go on will most likely be on the level of absorbing the correct forms used by the native speaker. However, if the non-native speaker is not motivated to improve his or her language, finding it adequate for its purpose, it will probably remain at the same level, give or take a few new items of vocabulary. This is known as fossilisation.

In some cases a parent may be totally uninterested in learning the other parent's language. Before the couple has children, this may never have been a problem – both speak either the majority language or another common language. If the minority language parent wants to introduce his or her own language for the first time when speaking to the baby, the other parent may quickly begin to feel left out. This may provide the necessary motivation to learn the language in question, or it may become a major source of friction in the family, and might even thwart the whole idea of exposing the child to both parents' languages.

For parents who want to be able to speak their own language to the child, this can be very frustrating. If the other parent does not support the use of the minority language it will be almost impossible to make it an active part of family life. Children will quickly detect any signs of disapproval from a parent. Some families find that the baby and the majority language parent learn the minority language together, but the child's vocabulary will generally accelerate away from the parent's by the age of 2. This can be minimised if the parent makes an active effort to learn the minority language.

Another option, which may in some cases be the only way to ensure that the child gets some input in the minority language is to arrange a system whereby the minority language-speaking parent speaks that language with the child in all situations except when the other parent is present.

'I'd recommend anyone in an international marriage should do their best to master their spouse's language or their host country's language, not only for the sake of their marriage, but also for the children's sake. We can't demand from our children anything which we parents cannot accomplish. So our children will be bilingual and bicultural to the extent that we ourselves are.'

(John Moore, Japan)

'Michael has always corrected all my mistakes (grammar and pronunciation), making me repeat the same words over and over again until I could pronounce them correctly. This has been very helpful, and it still is.'

(Stephanie Lysee, USA)

'Both my husband and I are language teachers – but we have found that it is best not to teach each other. Kenjiro will sometimes correct me – but I think he takes care not to do it automatically, but to consider the time, place, occasion, and most of all my mood – it can be irritating to be corrected when what is really important is making sure that the garbage gets taken out, for instance.'

(Robin Nagano, Japan)

Language mixing

Most people who live for many years away from countries where their native language is spoken as the majority language find that their native language is affected in one way or another. The most obvious consequence is that it is difficult to remember words in your native language. You may find that words of your second language pop up when you are speaking or writing in your native language. If you associate with other speakers of your native language who like yourself have lived for years with the second language, you may find yourselves throwing in words of the majority language when they seem particularly apt or just because they come to mind first. This is in addition to the times when you need to use a majority language word to refer to something which exists only in the country you live in. Since there is no risk of not being understood, this language mixing can sometimes be a real characteristic of this kind of speech.

> 'I find myself searching for words, and am most comfortable speaking with other long-term residents who also speak Japanese – and then we can mix in phrases without having to worry about it.'
>
> (Robin Nagano, Japan)

A family with two languages may in time develop their own hotchpotch of the two languages. The reasons for this are varied, but one reason is that parents might find it simpler to avoid minority language words that they know the child will not understand, using the majority language instead. Of course, if parents mix their languages in this way in the children's hearing, they should not be surprised if the children learn to do so too!

Mother: 'Let's go and pick some blåbär' (compare with 'Kom ska vi plocka blåbär' and 'Let's go and pick some bilberries').

Leif (4;0):   'Först ska jag climba upp, sen ska jag slida ner' (compare with 'First I'll climb up, then I'll slide down' and 'Först ska jag klättra upp, sen ska jag åka ner').

This is slightly different from the kind of mixing where the nouns and verbs of one language may be borrowed into the other language and given that language's endings, in much the same way as children with two languages do at a certain stage. This borrowing of English words into Swedish is a common feature of language used in computing and the like where people 'mejlar' (*skickar* send) email to each other and look at 'sajtar' (*webbplatser* sites) on the Internet.

Our children have found that from about the age of 10–12, their monolingual Swedish friends are likely to tease them about any mixing in of Swedish words in their English. This has given rise to a system whereby English is set as the only permissible language in, for example, the car on a ride to town for the so-called monolingual Swedish children as well as for those who have grown up with both languages. This game is thoroughly enjoyed by all. Obviously, this technique will not be helpful in all combinations of minority languages and countries of residence, but it works for us in Sweden where Swedish 12-year-olds can speak English well enough for informal conversation.

Language switching

An additional problem in the mixed language family may arise if any of them are in the habit of speaking the minority language in public: the family may be perceived as tourists in their own country. Even minority language speakers are probably quite fluent in the language of the country in which they live, and problems may arise if the minority language is reasonably well known as a school language, for example English or German in Sweden. The family risk being addressed in the minority language by well-meaning shop assistants. This puts them in the awkward situation of having to decide whether to answer in the majority language, embarrassing the shop assistants who may feel that they have been eavesdropping, or carrying on the conversation in the minority language without revealing that they are also proficient in the majority language.

Example

We generally speak English together, even in public. On one occasion we went into a bookshop in Uppsala, still talking together. We approached the counter and Una asked in good Swedish for a particular (English) title. We then followed the assistant to the shelf where he turned to Staffan and said in English 'I think this is the one you are looking for'. To say anything other than 'Thank you' would have been churlish. The assistant had obviously assumed that Una was speaking English with Staffan because he knew no Swedish.

'One problem that I have is that I don't like to speak English outside the home. When I speak English to my children, people assume that I don't know Hebrew (even though my children often answer in Hebrew) and they try to speak to me in English. I find this very aggravating, as my Hebrew is excellent and I don't want to sound or feel like an "outsider".'

(Bari Nirenberg, Israel)

Communication

Depending on the level of mastery that the non-native speaker has in the language spoken by the parents, communication may be more or less affected by the presence of two languages. Native speakers may find that they need to use relatively simple language when talking to their partner. There may be misunderstandings even when they both believe the non-native speaker has understood. A question like 'Do you know what I mean?' can be answered in the affirmative by someone who knows what they *think* you mean, without the misunderstanding ever becoming clear.

Of course, even using simple language becomes a habit, and does not really have to limit the level of conversation. It is possible to talk in simple terms about even the most complex matters if both parties are sufficiently interested. If parents usually talk to each other in the minority language, majority language speakers will most likely become very fluent in this language, in the sense of being able to speak at normal speed and without hesitation, even if their speech is accented and full of grammatical errors. This facilitates the couple's communication, making it less arduous for both parties.

Minority language families

Minority language families have two adults who are both speakers of the same language, but it is not the majority language in the society in which they live. In some ways, they have a much easier situation than the mixed language couple. Whether they originally met in their home country or in the country where they now live (or elsewhere), they have a lot in common. They form together an island of the minority language and culture in an ocean of foreignness. They can face the new culture and language in which they find themselves, and sometimes close the door on it and retire inside to a home life full of familiarity. The situation can vary depending upon the family's circumstances and the reason for their move.

Children in these families can make a clear distinction between the home and the world outside. A family who moves as a unit from one country to another to work brings a whole way of life with them. They expect to go on much as they did at home. They probably plan to go back to their country of origin after a number of years. Their position is not really that of immigrants who plan to make a new life in the new country, such as those Europeans who go to North America or New Zealand or Australia often do, but rather as temporary residents. These people are often well educated and work in universities or in multinational companies or organisations, such as the many American and British people working in the Swedish pharmaceutical industry or the international scene in the institutions and organisations of Brussels or Strasbourg. They may prefer to remain apart from the local community as far as possible, and place their children in international schools. They might not bother much with learning the local language unless it is necessary for their work, and may associate almost exclusively with others of their kind. They see themselves as ex-pats and keep closely in touch with what is going on at home, via newspapers, radio and satellite television. It is clear to them that they are living abroad, and they have no aspiration to become part of the society in which they are temporarily living.

Immigrants and refugees

There are many thousands of refugees in Europe, who have come from conflicts and disasters in many countries. They often intend to return to their own countries when the situation there improves, but may live in exile longer than they originally planned.

Refugee families often have the same kind of outlook on their stay in the new country as those who are in a country temporarily for work purposes. They may plan to return to their own country as soon as conditions improve, and so are not really interested in getting too involved with their new country. They have brought their language and culture with them. They may not feel motivated to learn the new language, and may find that their children are soon much better able to communicate with people in the new country than they are. The adults in such families often have extreme difficulty in getting any kind of employment in their new country, and if they do manage to get a job it is unlikely to correspond to their qualifications and capacity. These families often associate primarily with others like themselves and keep themselves informed about the situation in their homeland. Unfortunately, things do not always turn out according to plan. After a period of time has passed, it may become clear that the refugee family is unlikely to return home in the foreseeable future. Perhaps the political situation in their country of origin is not improving, or perhaps their children have become so firmly rooted in the soil of the host country that a move back home would be disastrous. At this point the family needs to take a fresh look at their situation in the new country, and maybe take steps to improve their skills in the language and look at their employment prospects. However, the very fact that there is an intact language and culture in the home is likely to ensure that the parents in the family will not become integrated into the society of the new country. The situation for their children is, of course, different. They will usually learn to master the language and culture fairly quickly, and may prefer and expect to live in the new country always.

This is the position for many refugees from Chile and other parts of Latin America living in Sweden. They did not expect to stay long in Sweden and settled down to live together, so that they rarely had any need to speak any language other than Spanish. Time went by, however, without any prospect of being able to return. The refugees' children attended Swedish schools and became fluent in Swedish, often acting as interpreters for their parents when they needed to communicate in Swedish with the authorities or doctors. Eventually, it became impossible to leave Sweden where the children had settled down. To then start learning Swedish after a number of years was impossible for many – it would have been like saying that they would never return to their home countries. In some countries, for example Germany and Sweden, there are thousands of immigrant workers who were brought in from Turkey and Greece and other countries during the 1960s and 1970s when there was work for everyone and jobs waiting for any ambitious person wanting to come and make their fortune. Many of these workers returned to their countries of origin, but quite a few settled permanently in their new countries. This kind of immigration has basically stopped in most countries.

Citizens of the EU are allowed to work in any of the other EU countries, and unemployed people may go to look for work elsewhere in the EU for three months without losing their unemployment benefit from home. Many do find work, despite a generally high level of unemployment in Europe. Others start their own businesses, and manage to make a living that way in a new country.

International employees

If, as is often the case, the family comes to the new country because one of the parents has got a job there, the other parent may or may not be allowed to work. Even if allowed to do so, the latter is unlikely to find a paying job on the open market, given the generally high level of unemployment. Some companies may have a scheme whereby accompanying spouses are able to work part time for the company, but this is not usually the case. This means that the working parent may easily be able to meet people and interact socially, while the other is left at home, often with children. Some international companies which recruit personnel from abroad take great pains to help accompanying families find their feet, others do nothing. Ideally the company should offer support at all stages, with locally employed staff specifically recruited to smooth the integration of newcomers from abroad.

Schools and pre-schools need to be investigated. There may be international schools available, where teaching is in the medium of English or other languages, which might be better for the children if the stay is not expected to be longer than a couple of years. Otherwise they may do better to learn the local language. This depends on the children's age and inclination. Some countries have systems whereby children can do their schoolwork by correspondence from the home country. Modern information technology and the Internet will probably do their bit to make this option better and more popular in the future. It may be possible for children to attend a local school part time, say four mornings a week, and concentrate on the work sent from the home-country school the rest of the time. This way they get the best of both worlds. The company should make information about this kind of arrangement available to their international employees.

Part of the fun in living abroad is the attraction of getting to know a new culture, and maybe learning a new language. Even though many international companies have English as their working language, knowledge of the local language can certainly make the stay more meaningful, particularly for the accompanying family members. It would be very helpful for the newcomers if the company held classes in the local language and culture.

Visiting academics

International companies may be reasonably motivated to look after their employees' welfare and ensure that the accompanying family adapts as well as possible. The situation can be a lot worse in other organisations, for example academic institutions. Typically universities make little or no effort to help their international undergraduates and postgraduates find their feet. They do even less for their families. In the case of visiting lecturers or professors they may help out with the task of finding accommodation, but this is usually done at the departmental level rather than through any central organisation.

The success of a period abroad depends to a great extent on how well the accompanying family adapts to their new surroundings. For the one who actually has the job, there is often not any problem, but the difficulty in getting to know people in a new country can be frustrating for an accompanying husband or wife who is trying to make the best of their new role as home-maker in a strange place. Of course, this is easier in some places than in others. But even in countries where people are chatty and open, it would be naive to believe that you are likely to slip into the local people's social life after a couple of months.

Many families in this position tend to centre their social life round others with the same linguistic and cultural background. Even those who have lived many years in the same country often find that they associate almost exclusively in their free time with other foreigners, even if they are not from the same country. The very fact that they are foreigners together is enough to give them something in common.

Chapter 2

Expecting a child in a bilingual home

Any couple's first child is awaited with a certain amount of trepidation. Nobody can be sure whether they will actually like parenthood or be able to do what is required until they have become parents. For the couple who live with two languages, for whatever reason, there are many additional questions. They must think through their linguistic situation and make a place in it for the child, just as they might prepare a corner of their bedroom for the baby's cradle.

What do you want for your child?

This is the most important question the prospective parents must ask themselves. Depending on the parents' circumstances and their plans for the future, they will regard different things as important. A couple who plan to stay only a few years in a country before returning to their mutual home country will want to plan differently from a family where one parent has immigrated permanently to the other's country, or parents who want their child to speak a language which neither of them speak natively where a second language is introduced artificially. Some of the following considerations may be relevant.

Speaking an immigrant parent's language

Even if you have married a foreigner and moved to his or her country to make your life together, you probably want to ensure that your child learns your language, and not just the majority language which almost everybody around you speaks. It is enough to live with a speaker of another language: you may not want to raise one! Of course, your child will learn the majority language, but it need not be from you, at least not in the early stages. Many parents living outside a country where their own language is spoken feel that being able to speak their own language to their children is a vital part of their relationship. No matter how well you know the majority language, it can be difficult to talk to a tiny baby in that language, to sing and play and scold and comfort without the resources learned in your own childhood.

However, if the parents decide for whatever reason that one or both of them should speak to the child in a language other than their own, it can be done, although there may be a price to pay in the relationship between parent and child in later years. A mother faced with a rebellious teenager may be better equipped to counter defiance and rhetoric in her own language, and will perhaps command more respect and credibility in the child's eyes than if she is a less-than-perfect speaker of the majority language which the child probably masters totally.

Some mixed language families arrange for the minority language to be spoken by both parents to the child, at least at home. This solution means that one parent speaks a non-native language to the child, at least some of the time, and may feel awkward. The relationship between parents and children is so special, that it is a shame to introduce what some may perceive as a barrier – a non-native language. However, this solution gives the minority language a head start, which will let the child become more competent in that language in the early years. Some parents are concerned that their children may be at a disadvantage if they do not speak or understand the majority language very well before starting kindergarten or pre-school, but experience shows that children are exceptional language learners and usually catch up. The warnings that have been raised have generally concerned children from communities where there is little opportunity to hear native speakers of the majority language.

In cases where one parent is equally at home with both languages, other options are open, for example, that that parent can speak either language with the child, depending on who else is present. Parents who have themselves grown up with two languages may well feel they want to interact with their child in both their languages.

Belonging to a minority group in the country of residence

If the family's minority language is spoken by many people in the same area, so that it is meaningful to talk about an immigrant or ex-pat community, it may be important that the child is able to become part of that community. The family's social life may be spent largely within such a group, so that the child needs to know enough of the minority language to be able to participate in various activities, such as going to religious services, play-group and maybe Saturday school or even ordinary school through the medium of that language.

> 'Like many immigrants, we socialised in the well-established Armenian ethnic community in New York. I attended Saturday Armenian school and therefore was literate as well.'
>
> (Suzanne Hovanesian, USA)

Other examples of this kind of minority community are the Finnish community in Sweden, the Greek–Cypriot community in London or the English community in Brussels. Members of these communities tend to have a lot of contact with each other and many activities are aimed at passing on the minority language and culture to the children.

Feeling at home in the immigrant parent's home country

Many people who have emigrated will want to return regularly to their home country to visit friends and relatives and to keep a lingering homesickness at bay. Sometimes immigrants may hunger for the feeling of being as fully linguistically and culturally competent as they were before they left their native country. The feeling can in part be recreated by a visit to that country, although both the country and the individual will have changed in the intervening years. Immigrants may wish for their children to feel at home in the country that they themselves once left. They may even wish for their children to live in that country in the future, or at least to study there or choose a marriage partner from there. This can be a major reason for some parents ensuring that their children become proficient in the minority language.

> 'I would raise my children speaking Spanish, so they don't lose their cultural background. It kills me to see Hispanic children not knowing their native tongue. Now I know how my parents felt.'
>
> (Marc Rod, Florida)

'I am very much aware of how much of my culture they do not share. They know the geography and social life of Ireland from their summers there. They know Irish music from recordings and from the fact that I have a number of musician friends, some of whom are very well known. They associate Irish music with me (once when I was away in China, they asked their mother to put a recording of Irish music on because they missed me).'

(Sean Golden, Barcelona)

Being able to communicate with relatives

If an immigrant parent still has family members in the country of origin, it is important that the child can communicate with these people. Not only is it tragic if grandparents cannot speak to their grandchildren, but also it can be important for the child to realise that the immigrant parent also has a background and a family.

'I spoke less and less German once I entered school and did not speak any at all, except isolated words or greetings, from about age 8 till 14. That spring my German grandparents visited and I was very ashamed at not being able to speak with them.'

(William C. Brown, Delaware)

'There came a moment when they were about 4–5 years old when they rebelled and complained bitterly about my addressing them in English (I was the only father who did so, it made them feel "different", etc.). They said no one else around us spoke English. Fortunately, this happened in June, just before we went to Ireland, where they would be together with their grandparents and aunts and uncles, and I could remind them that, in Ireland, nobody around them spoke Spanish, and that their grandparents wouldn't understand them if they spoke in Spanish.'

(Sean Golden, Barcelona)

In the case of a mixed marriage where one partner is from the country of residence, the children's picture of their parents' childhood can be very unbalanced. The children might meet their grandparents, uncles, aunts and cousins on, say, the father's side very often, perhaps even daily. They might even live in the same house as their father grew up in, go to the same school as their father, play in the same places and swim at the same beaches. The father will be able to share his childhood with his children in a very concrete way. If the mother gets no opportunity to share her upbringing with her children, they may get the impression that she has no background; that she just appeared fully grown out of the earth, without the substance of family behind her. It can be very important for the mother in such a situation that the children have the linguistic and cultural competence to be able to form real relationships with members of her family, and to be able to participate fully in whatever is happening on visits to the mother's home country.

Absolute balanced bilingualism or getting by?

Some couples, especially those who do not have much contact with other bilingual families, talk of bringing up their children to be bilingual, by which they may mean to be equally competent in two languages, and to be indistinguishable from monolingual native speakers in both languages. This is, in our opinion, an unrealistic ambition in many cases, if the family does not spend almost equal amounts of time in countries where the languages are spoken. Balanced bilingualism means that both languages are equally strong. This is often difficult to achieve while the children are small, but may not be unachievable in the long term in some cases, given sufficient motivation on the part of the children themselves. Many parents in mixed and minority language families report that their children's dominance in the languages involved goes in waves. The minority language may be stronger while they are small, while the other takes over when they start school. The minority language may be temporarily stronger during extended trips to a country where it is spoken, only to be put back into place on the return home.

Children growing up with the majority language as dominant may become more balanced if they later spend a term or a year at school in a country where the minority language is spoken. There are many exchange schemes, both within Europe and elsewhere, which arrange for youngsters to spend a period abroad, living in a family in the host country. These schemes may require the exchange student's family to act as hosts for a young person from another country for an equivalent period of time. A young person who has grown up with the language of the host country as a second language has a chance to develop full competence in the language at this stage. This opportunity is not usually available to those who learned the language only as a foreign language at school. Only the most exceptionally talented among such students will be able to speak the language of the host country without a foreign accent. There is reason to believe that young people who have been exposed to two languages from a very young age can learn to speak both languages without a foreign accent.

Parents who expected their children to be indistinguishable from monolingual native speakers may be disappointed to hear their child speak the minority language with a foreign accent, or with obvious interference from the majority language. Languages in contact generally influence each other, and the problem may become less in time if the child receives sufficient input in both languages. Time spent in an environment where only the minority language is heard is very valuable.

Even worse is if the children have interference the other way, from the minority language to the majority language, especially if the majority language is their dominant language (as it usually is for school-age children, unless they are being schooled in the minority language). It is important for everybody to fully master one language, regardless of how many other languages they know. Children who are experiencing difficulty in their dominant language need help to work on the problem areas, be they vocabulary, syntax or pronunciation. It may be necessary to get expert help from a speech therapist, or other person, if one can be found with experience of bilingual families, but parents can themselves help their children if they are aware that there is a problem. Suggestions for supporting a child's linguistic development will be found in Appendix B.

An advantage for adult life

Some parents see their children's prospective bilingualism as an asset for the future, almost as a qualification which will be useful to the children in their careers. This is particularly so if the language the children stand to learn has high status in the country in which the family live. There is more currency in the notion of English, Spanish or French being valuable for the children in their future careers than there is for languages such as Swedish, Catalan or Latvian, although, since nobody can tell what the future has in store for us or our children, you never know! Having access to a second language might be enough to build a career on, particularly if the language is less well known and not usually studied by speakers of the other language. In such a case, the young person with an excellent command of two languages may be in a strong position.

In an effort to give the child an advantageous start in life some parents take steps to expose their child to a second language which is not a native language for either of them. This can be done by placing the child in an international school or an immersion language programme, where the language of instruction is new to the child, by employing a foreign au-pair to be with the children, or by having one or both of the parents speak a language which is not their native language with the child, either only at home or in all situations.

Making plans

Before the birth of their first child the couple who want to bring their child up with two languages or who themselves have two languages should think about and discuss the way they envisage their child's linguistic development. They need to think about who is going to speak which language to the child, and whether this will change according to the situation: whether they are at home or not, which country they are in, whether there are monolingual guests present, and so on. All this should be decided before the child is born because for many people it is extremely difficult to change the language you speak to a person once you have established a relationship in one language.

It may be helpful to meet and discuss with others who are in a similar linguistic situation, especially if they have older children. Much can be learned just by spending time in such a family. Ask them how they arrange their use of the two languages, what rules or habits they have for who speaks what to whom in which situation, what problems they have encountered and how they have dealt with them. Look at how their children speak and understand the two languages. Later on at home you may want to discuss whether what you saw was the way you want things to turn out for your child. Learn from what the others did wrong, or if you want things to turn out differently, try to find a way to make that happen for your child, given what you learned from the other family.

Try to get others to share their experiences with you. Join the Bilingual Families Internet mailing list (biling-fam) if you have Internet access at home or at work. You can ask questions of other parents there, and maybe even share your experiences with someone else. This and other Internet resources are listed in Appendix D.

After you have decided together how you want to arrange your child's exposure to the two languages, it might be a good idea to talk to both sets of grandparents about your plans. Grandparents are frequently conservative, and may be against the whole idea of bringing up the child with two languages. They may advise you to let the child concentrate on one language at a time or to completely forget the idea of 'confusing' the child with the minority language at all. This kind of advice is more likely to come from majority language grandparents who feel that they will be able to communicate with the child whatever happens.

Families who are temporarily abroad may be advised to try to return to their home country before their child starts school or pre-school to 'spare' the child the trouble of ever having to learn more than a smattering of the majority language. You may be better able before the birth to explain the reasoning behind your decision to bring up your children with two languages in just the way you have planned. Experts may also offer advice, although they may not be well informed about bilingualism.

'We had difficulties with the day-care centre when the oldest attended, and they kept trying to persuade me not to speak English as this was "bad for her development". But both my husband and I ignored them and tried to convince them of the value of two languages from the start.'

(Nancy Holm, Sweden)

'When my brother started school [he's older], a teacher told my parents not to worry about him being able to pick up English; that my parents should speak to him in our native language [Taiwanese] at home, and that the English would come at school. So, my parents speak both Taiwanese and English to us and I am VERY grateful. I can communicate with my relatives without an interpreter and can independently traverse throughout Taiwan.'

(Linda Lee, USA)

'Unfortunately, when we returned to the States, some jerk of a child psychologist told us to cease using French in her presence since it might disturb her little psyche. She has been in France and other

> Francophonic environments since, but still hesitates to use French in our presence. Like when she was a pre-schooler: "Vas au lit." "I don't want to go to bed".'
>
> (Merton Bland, USA)

Family life with two languages is easier than it looks. For those outside the situation of the bilingual family looking in, the complex of rules and conventions regulating who in the family speaks which language to other family members and the way these patterns change in the company of others looks daunting. But those involved are very used to the situation. For the children, language switching is as natural as breathing. After all, even in monolingual relationships every pair of people uses a different 'language': you do not speak in the same way to your husband as to your son, nor to your doctor as to your mother. The only difference in the bilingual set-up is that the various relationships require more than one language to be used.

A couple of weeks before the birth of our first child we happened to sit next to a mixed language family in a café. Of course, we had to eavesdrop. After quite a long while we managed to work out the rules. The father was an English speaker, and everybody except the mother spoke English to him and he answered in English. The mother was a Swedish speaker, and the children spoke Swedish to her, and were answered in Swedish. The parents spoke Swedish together. When you know how it works, the conversation of a mixed language family is perfectly logical, but for outsiders listening to it, the arrangement looks confusing and chaotic. The constant switching of languages according to who is speaking to whom might seem less orderly than it usually is.

What is in a name?

In the context of the mixed language couple, names take on a new significance. The decision of what names the individuals involved will use after marriage depends partly on the laws of the country in which the couple lives. Whether a woman chooses to adopt her husband's surname or keep her maiden name might be very important to her, if not in the first flush of married bliss then perhaps later when she finds her foreign surname a burden and perhaps an imposition.

In some countries, it is possible for the woman to keep her own name and also acquire her husband's name, giving a double-barrelled variant, in which case the name, for example Una Cunningham-Andersson, gives a thumbnail sketch of the story of its bearer's life. Unfortunately this kind of name may have an upper-class ring to it in some parts of the English-speaking world. In other countries it is not the custom for women to change their name at all on marriage. Sometimes it is possible for the man to take the woman's surname on marriage, although this option tends not to be as popular. The couple must reach their own decision within the options available to them. In our case, Una has recently dropped Andersson from her name after using it for 17 years.

The question of what to name the children of intercultural marriages can be even more controversial. Fortunately it is usually possible to give a child two or even more forenames, so that both cultures are represented. The names given to the child may be chosen in accordance with this, giving combinations which may not go well together, but serve the purpose of reflecting the child's background. An alternative is to give the child names which work in both languages: English, Swedish or Spanish speakers could name a child David or Daniel and have a name which looks native for all concerned when it is written, even if the pronunciation is somewhat different in each language. Parents often try to predict where they are likely to spend most of their time while the children are growing up and ensure that names are unremarkable in that country. Other parents might like to choose a name from the other culture, to give an unusual name in the country of residence. There are different ways of rationalising the difficult process of choosing names for children, and parents can only hope that their children will not hold their choice of name against them.

There are many advantages to ensuring that children have a reasonable and useful name, wherever they end up. One way to achieve this is to give them several names. Different countries will have different legislation about the number of names a child can be given and about which of them can be used to address the child. In Sweden you can give a child any number of names, but you will have to specify which of these is to be used to address the child, although this can later be changed fairly easily.

Our take on this was to give our children three names each – at least one that was very ordinary in Swedish, at least one that was very ordinary in English and a bonus name that was from one or other of our families. So far, our children have been happy to be called by the names we chose to address them by, except for Anders who at the age of 12 chose to be known as John, his second name, at school. This has led to some confusion, since he continues to be known as Anders outside school, and the two worlds do sometimes meet.

'We knew we were going to live in Mexico and gave our kids Spanish first names. This makes for a more comfortable environment for them.'

(R. Chandler-Burns, Mexico)

Be prepared!

There are some aspects of parenthood in a bilingual family that may come as a surprise to those involved. For example, a parent speaking the minority language to a child is very conspicuous. It may be unpleasant at first to see heads turn when you say something to your child in the hearing of strangers. As long as the mixed language family is just a couple, then they probably do not attract much attention in public. Many immigrant parents find that they do not become conspicuous until they are out with their children. This is particularly so if the parent and child do not look 'foreign', for example, a Dutch mother in Germany, a Finnish father in Norway, or a Spanish mother in Italy. To the casual onlooker it may then come as a surprise to hear that the parent and child speak another language. They 'look' as though they ought to speak German, Norwegian or Italian or whatever. If onlookers also get to know that the parent can actually speak the majority language perfectly well, it may seem absurd to be speaking another language to the child, particularly if the child is too little to understand much of what is being said. For most people foreign languages are difficult and it may be quite incomprehensible to them that a tiny child can learn more than one language. This may lead to open criticism of the parent or unsolicited advice, which can be just as unpleasant.

'People (strangers) usually have two reactions when they hear me and the child speak English in public (how could I ever refrain myself and adopt another linguistic posture?). Most people will smile and attempt to say something like "what's your name?" etc. and will ask if he understands Portuguese – so far, both mother and child are "tolerated" because I do speak Portuguese and always stress that he understands Portuguese – which pleases people no end and somehow softens their (yes, occasional) attitude of "these foreigners who think they can just walk about in our country without speaking

Portuguese!" On other occasions people will "marvel" at the child's ability to "perform" in two languages, but I will always explain that children are like sponges and will learn anything given the opportunity.'

(Ana Cristina Gabriel, Lisbon)

In some families the children will hate the attention that the public use of the minority language generates, and will avoid the situation as much as possible. Others will not mind, or even feel proud of their linguistic prowess. Of course, the level of attention will depend on the setting. In cosmopolitan areas it is not unusual to hear foreign languages. Passers-by in other places may make disparaging comments to the effect that 'When you're here speak . . .'. There has been a heated discussion on this topic on the Bilingual Families Internet mailing list (see Appendix D). The group was divided into those who hold that speaking a language which is not understood by those within hearing is akin to exposing them to the smoke of your cigarette, and those who believe that they have every right to speak whatever language they please in every situation. Obviously, the reaction to speaking a minority language in public will depend on several things:

- The listeners may not be used to hearing a foreign language spoken at all.
- They may have a generally negative attitude to all things foreign.
- They may have a particularly negative attitude to speakers of the language in question.
- They may feel that they are being talked about.
- They may feel that visitors, and particularly immigrants, should learn and exclusively use the majority language, even with each other. In this case they might view it as particularly unsuitable to pass on the foreign language to a child.

Another, perhaps unexpected, aspect of new parenthood is that the parent who has to change from the language spoken by the couple to the language he or she is to speak to the child may be reluctant to do so, despite the plans laid down by the couple before the birth.

Examples

A Spanish man and French woman live in Spain. They speak the minority language, French, together. Before their child is born, they decide that they will each speak their own language to the child, in all situations. When the child was born, his father felt very strange switching from French to Spanish for the sake of a tiny baby who understood nothing he said. At the insistence of his wife, he persevered, and continued speaking Spanish to his son.

A Greek man and English woman living in England had much the same experience. The Greek man was to speak Greek to his daughter, but felt unable to switch to Greek, especially since he did not use Greek otherwise except with adult Greek speakers and in Greece. As a result, the child did not grow up speaking Greek, but her mother arranged for her to receive lessons in Greek from a private teacher from the age of 6. She is now able to speak enough to communicate with her Greek grandmother. Her father has become more interested in speaking Greek to her.

In some cases a minority language may be the only clue that its speaker belongs to an oppressed or unpopular group. In such cases parents must decide how they and their children will use the languages. There are undoubtedly situations where discretion is required and where children need to learn that their minority language is not always viewed positively. For example, this situation is faced by American English speakers in certain parts of the Middle East or German speakers in some parts of Europe. Parents who succeed in helping their children to acquire the minority language in such circumstances are to be admired. In the years since September 2001 the position of Moslems and other peoples from the Middle East in the Western world has changed and this has led to difficulties for many people living in the West who wish to bring up their children as speakers of Arabic, Persian, Kurdish or any of a multitude of other languages spoken in that part of the world. Whether or not the family is Moslem they may meet negative attitudes which in some cases lead to the parents choosing to speak the majority language in public, and maybe even at home. This will inevitably make it extremely difficult for the children to acquire the parents' language.

> ' "Raising children bilingually" isn't so pretty when your home language is hated. Keeping your minority status isn't easy when you know it's going to cause your kids problems, and it's worse if your minority has ever been the object of genocide – the case of Indians, Jews, Gypsies and many others.'
>
> (Anonymous, Mexico)

Reactions from the folk back home

The news that their grown-up son or daughter has 'taken up with a foreigner' might come as a shock for many parents, particularly if the son or daughter concerned lives in the home country. Even if the foreigner concerned is a fellow European and there is no major racial difference, the thought of the cultural and linguistic problems ahead may seem daunting. Many worry about their prospective grandchildren and wonder if such a relationship can ever be successful. They may wonder if they will be able to communicate with the boyfriend or girlfriend, and dread the prospect of their child moving to another country. Accepting a foreigner into the family is often a challenge for the older generation on both sides.

The extended family of cousins, grandparents, uncles and aunts on both sides may have mixed feelings about the family's way of dealing with the two languages they live with. On the one hand, the first child of the family may be watched closely for signs that this business of two languages is just too much to expect from a baby. On the other hand, the side or sides of the family representing the minority language (one or both sets of grandparents) may well be worried about not being able to communicate at all with their grandchildren if they do not learn to speak their language. If the children manage to learn enough of the minority language to build up a relationship with their grandparents, this will probably be appreciated, although some grandparents can be insensitive enough to criticise the children's hard-won skills as not being native-like.

This kind of remark can be hurtful to the parent who has often single-handedly helped the children acquire their minority language skills. Bear in mind that grandparents may be deeply disappointed that their son or daughter lives far away from them in another country; they may be unfamiliar with the culture and traditions of the country in which their child and grandchildren live. If their grandchildren's other parent is from that country, this can also be a source of sorrow to the grandparents.

'In trying to maintain a bilingual household, it has had an impact on my wife's family. They all think it is great!!! My mother-in-law, sister-in-law and brother-in-law have taken up Spanish.'

(Dr Edgar Monterroso, USA)

'Our parents sometimes think we've done our children a disservice by raising them in a second culture and language.'

(Joyce Roth, Japan)

If the majority language spoken in the country where the children live is a high prestige language, especially if it is a school language for children in the country where the minority language is spoken, such as French is in England, and English is in Sweden, the emigrant parent may come upon envy from his or her own siblings who feel that their children are not being given such an advantageous upbringing, with the chance to acquire a second language with what looks like no effort at all. Their children will instead have to learn the 'hard' way, at school with grammar exercises and vocabulary lists, with presumably less chance of success. The work put into living with two languages by parents and children alike is not immediately observable from the outside.

Chapter 3

The family language system

Developing a system

According to their circumstances a family will develop a system regulating the use of the two languages with which they live. When the circumstances change in some way, the system must be flexible enough to meet the requirements made of it. When a mixed language couple first meet they will decide actively, or by default, which language to speak. As time goes on, that decision might need revising; perhaps another solution becomes more appropriate when a child is born, or when the child needs help with majority language homework. A divorce, moving to another country or a new member of the family (maybe granny moves in) might require changes in the family's language set-up. A family which has chosen for both parents to use the minority language at home might want to reconsider this decision if they move to a country where that language is the majority language. Then the former majority language needs a place to be spoken if it is to be kept alive. Of course, if neither of the parents are native speakers of that language they may have no need or wish to keep up their own or their children's skills in the language.

Example

A family with a Swedish father and an American mother lived for many years in Sweden, where both the mother and father spoke English at home to the children. Outside the home, the father spoke his native Swedish to the children, while the mother continued to speak English to the children in all situations. When the family went to live in the USA for two years, they needed to ensure that the children's Swedish was kept up, both for the sake of their communication with their Swedish relatives, and since they knew they would be returning after two years. They tried to switch to everybody speaking Swedish at home, but it did not work for two reasons. First, the mother did not feel comfortable speaking Swedish to the children at all: she had never done so and her Swedish (which had never been that good) was rapidly weakening while away from Sweden. Second, the father was required to work long hours and was often away from home from early morning to late evening, and rarely saw his children during the week. He was not around to speak Swedish to either his wife or his children. The result was that by the time the family moved back to Sweden the children were monolingual in English, and seemed to have forgotten all the Swedish they had ever known. Fortunately, it gradually came back to them once they got back to school and got into the way of things Swedish again. Now the children are very competent in both languages.

The language chosen by brothers and sisters to talk between themselves is usually the majority language if this is their dominant language (as is usual, at least for children of school age). Sometimes parents may try to persuade their children to talk in the minority language together, but it is difficult to influence others' choice of language, and in any case, it is not really any of the parents' business. It may be that the minority language has a greater chance of being used between siblings if it is the only language spoken by both parents at home, but even this is not always any help. Sometimes older siblings address a younger one in the minority language if they believe it might get better results (perhaps sounding more authoritative, i.e. more like Mum or Dad) or if they perceive the younger child as understanding the minority language better (which may well be the case).

Example

Leif (9;5) to Pat (3;10): 'Ge mig den Pat, give it to me!'

Language and personality

It is an unavoidable fact of life with two languages that everyone in the family who speaks the minority language also sometimes has to speak the majority language, unless the family lives in a self-contained ex-pat or immigrant environment. Even parents who always speak the minority language in all situations when speaking directly to their children will sometimes have to use the majority language to others in the presence of their children. For small children it can be confusing to hear their mother change languages when talking, say, to a shop assistant. So much alters when we switch languages: some languages are spoken in a higher tone of voice than others; the amount of pitch movement may change; a speaker might speak with lower volume in one language than another, for cultural reasons or because of uncertainty, which can make the speaker appear less self-assured. It may seem to small children that their mother alters her personality when she changes language, particularly if they are not used to hearing her do so.

In fact, some aspects of a speaker's personality do seem to change when switching from a native language to a non-native language. In a language which is not completely mastered, speakers do not have access to stylistic variation and nuances of meaning. Speech may become hesitant and uncertain, which gives the impression that speakers are unsure about what they are saying. It is difficult to win an argument elegantly in a second language. This is an important reason why parents need to think carefully before giving up their own language when talking to their children. They are likely to lose prestige in the eyes of their children if they are not fully competent in the language they use to speak to them. Ultimately this may lead to a lack of respect which might have been avoided if parents had been able to stick to their own language in all dealings with their children.

Parents with two languages

People who have grown up with two languages may want to pass both languages on to their children. This may not be altogether easy, depending on the family's make-up and circumstances. A young man who grew up in, say, Spain with an English mother and a Spanish father will probably speak much more native-like Spanish than English. If he marries a Spanish woman and they make their home in Spain, he may want his children to learn his second language, English. His mother may be very keen to help, not wanting to have to speak Spanish to her grandchildren. There may, however, be difficulties if he does not feel confident enough speaking English to his children. In addition, his Spanish wife may not be in favour of introducing a second language at all, not really perceiving her husband as anything but a Spaniard.

Whether this kind of arrangement works out depends on how motivated the parents are to help their children learn the minority language. If the children are to achieve a reasonable degree of proficiency, steps must be taken to ensure that they are exposed to the language frequently, either through their grandparents or other people.

'I have children and grandchildren. I brought them up in one language only – Hebrew. Although my husband and I occasionally speak Dutch, we did not think this was an important language, and thus decided not to teach our children Dutch. However, I did think of the importance of English, but my husband was not very good at English, so it would have been "artificial" if we had spoken English together.'

(Yedida Heymans, Israel)

'Any children of ours would grow up multilingual too. My husband, in spite of being American, also speaks Korean, and has picked up a fair number of Dutch words and phrases and some Farsi through contact with my parents. We would probably talk to them in the same linguistic hodge-podge I had growing up; I know from personal experience that children can sort it out and limit the domain of each when necessary.'

(Jasmin Harvey, USA)

'As a translator, I know how difficult it is to speak one's mother tongue properly, how the language constantly evolves (my five-year-old dictionary has become obsolete), and how important it is to give a child the proper tools to learn to appreciate his mother tongue, the richness and the classics of it *before* he decides to learn another language. If you impose on the child another language, he will not have the time (or he will lose the desire) to explore his mother tongue. Twenty-four hours in a day, less eight hours' sleep, less eating and playing with other kids... I mean, give the poor kid a break. The real issue is: What is better? To really learn and explore one language, or to approximately communicate in two?'

(Jacques Clau, Canada)

One person—one language

For many years the one person—one language method of raising children bilingually has been recommended to mixed language couples as the most suitable. The main principle is that the parents each speak their own language to their children. The children are then expected to answer their parents in the language the parents use to them. For some parents this is the only conceivable way to manage the situation. If neither parent is prepared to surrender the privilege of speaking their language to their child, then this is the way to go about life in a mixed language family. There are, however, potential problems with this method. If the parent who represents the minority language is not with the children much, they may not get enough input in this language. This may lead to them never really getting started with the minority language.

> 'My idea then was that the OPOL [one person—one language] method was the best from what I had heard so we decided that I would speak French to Alienor and Wendy would speak Chinese to her. What we had not figured though was that the little time I could spend with Alienor would not be enough for her to get a fair dose of French. I must say that I have a fulltime job with long hours and that on top of that I work two or three weekends a month on freelance translations which does keep me busy. When I have some free time, the first thing that comes to my mind is to relax, and interacting in French with my children when they don't always understand what I say sometimes does not feel very relaxing to me.'
>
> (Alain Fontaine, Taiwan)

An additional problem may arise with the one person—one language method if the parents do not both understand the other's language. It is possible to feel quite left out of conversations between the child and the other parent if you do not understand what they are saying. One solution to this problem is for the parent to improve their knowledge of the other parent's language. There will otherwise be difficulties when the family is assembled. If the parents do understand each other's language, then it is possible for one to pick up a conversational thread started by the other, switching languages as they go.

Leif (9;7):	'I want to go to town soon.'
Mother:	'We'll be going sometime this week.'
Father:	'Vad vill du göra där?' ('What do you want to do there?')

The one person–one language method requires that the speaker establishes contact with the appropriate listener before beginning to speak. It is not really possible to make a remark intended for both parents, although children must, of course, sometimes find a way round that problem. Our experience is that the children ensure that the appropriate parent is listening before starting to say what they want to, by first saying 'Mamma!' or 'Pappa!' and waiting for an answer. If the remark is intended for both parents they will sometimes check the other parent's understanding by asking a follow-on question of that parent.

Suzanne Romaine (1995: 186) writes that a very common outcome of the one person–one language method is a child who can understand the languages of both parents but speaks only the language of the community in which they live. She goes on to say that sociolinguistic studies have shown that it is very difficult for children to acquire active command of a minority language where that language does not receive support from the community. Arnberg (1987: 35–42) confirms this with the results of a study of Swedish–English-speaking children in Sweden who by the age of 7 would all answer their mothers in Swedish, although they were willing to speak English to the experimenter. The parents expressed disappointment at their children's lack of fluency in English. The children were, however, able to converse in English when motivated to do so. In some of the families who described their situations to us, the children even began to avoid the parent who speaks their weaker language with them.

'At the moment my daughter prefers to be spoken to in English. Sometimes I am very tempted to use English because she seems to respond much better to English. Whenever both of us go to pick our daughter up from the childcare she wants to go straight to my husband and absolutely refuses to come to me. We are not sure why. Some say because girls often like fathers more. We suspect that the fact I speak Japanese to her may cause this reaction. She might not like to be spoken to in Japanese. Even at home she wants to be with him rather than with me. Especially when she is tired.'

(Kaori Matsuda, Australia)

> 'Prior to kindergarten, we spoke English with them, but of course they picked up Japanese from their playmates. After entering kindergarten, the balance of Japanese/English shifted to Japanese. I spoke Japanese with the children because that's the more difficult one and they needed help with school. My husband's Japanese wasn't very good, so the children tended to avoid speaking with him when they were primary age.'
>
> (Joyce Roth, Japan)

There are, however, success stories, such as those reported in Saunders (1982) and Döpke (1992). Romaine (1995) comments that the success stories concern minority languages which are not stigmatised and children from an advantaged background. Arnberg (1987: 43) points out that most studies of successful bilingualism are made by linguists concerning their own children. Saunders (1988: 33) rejects the notion that only middle-class families can succeed in raising children with two languages, offering evidence from a study he has made concerning a Turkish labourer who successfully raised his two daughters in Australia as competent Turkish/English bilinguals (Saunders 1984).

Our own experience of the one person–one language method is very positive so far. Our children are spoken to in the minority language, English, by their mother and in the majority language, Swedish, by their father. All of them will now always answer in the language in which they are addressed, and their English is no longer laced with Swedish words. They can and will speak more careful English to monolingual English speakers, just like the children in Arnberg's work. Leif's English cannot be described as native-like at 16;9, but he handles the language well and is frequently asked to guide foreign visitors to the agricultural college he attends because his ease and skills far exceed those of his monolingual peers. His Swedish is native. Anders has, from about the age of 7, been very particular about keeping the languages separate, sometimes asking for vocabulary before he starts speaking. Now, at 14;10, his English vocabulary has no obvious gaps. He has attended an English-medium school for the past couple of years and that has enabled his English to develop to a point where he can be described as native in both languages. In fact, subtle phonetic measurements suggest that he appears to be dominant in English (Cunningham 2003). At 6;5 Pat spoke only Swedish, although he understood English as well as Swedish. Now at 11;0 he will use the languages appropriately, answering in English when addressed in English, although his English syntax and pronunciation are not native-like. His Swedish is native. Elisabeth is now 9;5 and attends a bilingual (English/Swedish) class and appears to be perfectly balanced in her languages (Cunningham 2003) and indeed to have above average (for native speakers) skills for her age in both languages. The children were all English-dominant until they started pre-school at around 3 years of age. They all had a period of Swedish dominance when they started pre-school and school and for Elisabeth and Anders, that has changed since they entered bilingual or English-medium schooling, leaving them native-like in both languages.

'I think the advantage is that the child(ren) can associate one language system to one parent and can sort two languages out in their mind in early stages of their life. Disadvantage is that I (or my husband) have to be rude to our guests who are monolingual. Even in public (such as in shops, child care, etc.) I sometimes feel slightly awkward speaking in minority language.'

(Kaori Matsuda, Australia)

'I never spoke English with my kids – I was very principled about that aspect of the learning process.'

(Andreas Schramm, Minnesota)

'When our second child was learning to talk, she used to look at a new person, put her hands on her head and say, "Head". If she didn't get a response, she would say, "Huvud". Usually people would respond with hands, feet, tummy. It was her way of screening what language she should try with them.'

(American mother in Sweden)

'Every person should speak always only one (and the same) language with the children when they are very young. (I have heard about children growing with three or four languages if they can associate a determinate person with a determinate language.) Another important thing is to have at least two adults speaking the "minority" language with the child and between themselves. After discussing these problems with other bilingual families we came to the conclusion that the child needs to hear "a dialogue". Perhaps this is the reason my children never refused to speak Slovak in public as often happens. (My mother used to stay with us for long periods and we also spent our holidays in Slovakia.)'

(Elena Bertoncini, Italy)

'My expectations have been met, and exceeded. My daughter can switch back and forth between French and English with ease and speed. I'm satisfied with how bilingualism is working within our family.'

(Leslie Yee, Canada)

The one parent–one language method usually means that the child is introduced to both languages from birth. Some parents and others feel that two languages at once is too much for a tiny baby to deal with. They are afraid that the child will end up completely confused without real competence in either language. These fears may be fuelled by observing young children at a certain stage of bilingual development who freely mix the languages, and even older children who mix the languages in certain circumstances. However, young children, despite a period of confusion and frustration, seem to get it all sorted out if they get enough input in both languages, even if the parents are not especially consistent. The older children learn that they can mix the languages for ease of communication or for effect with others who share their linguistic background, but they soon learn to keep the languages 'pure' when around monolinguals, at least at the lexical (word) level, even if they still have interference from the majority language in their grammar and pronunciation of the minority language.

Such parents may choose not to speak the minority language at all to their child, planning to introduce it later, when the child has become competent in the majority language. The problem with this plan is that it is very difficult to change the language you use to speak to a person, and older children are not likely to appreciate being spoken to in a language they do not understand; they will have to be 'taught' the language first. It is much easier with tiny babies who do not expect to understand what they hear.

Some families may choose not to speak their language with their children because they wish the child to become assimilated totally in the majority culture. In the past, parents were often advised not to speak their own language to their children. It is now generally thought that this advice was misguided. Children can manage very well with the majority language if they just get enough input from native speakers. If a lot of their majority language input is from non-native speakers, they may have influences from those speakers in their majority language speech. In addition, older children may come to feel ashamed of or look down on their parents if they speak the majority language poorly, especially if that is the language the parents use with the children. It is a shame to deny children access to their parents' language and culture. Later in life the children will perhaps lament never having learned their parents' language, and may feel cut off from part of their heritage.

It happens fairly often in mixed language families that the parents start off each speaking their own languages to the children, but eventually drift into using the majority language together. This seems to be more likely to happen if the parents use the majority language when speaking to each other, so that the minority language parent only has to shift into that language to speak to the children. If the children go through a stage (temporary or permanent) of answering the minority language parent in the majority language it is easy to go on in that language, which is the children's dominant language. The parent may then give up what feels like an uphill struggle to impose a language on reluctant children, and stop using the minority language altogether or use it sporadically. This result can feel like a failure all round. If it is at all possible it may be better to carry on using the minority language to the children, even if they respond in the majority language: they will be learning passive skills just by listening, and passive knowledge of a language can easily become active on a trip to a country where the language is spoken.

'When I remind her to ask her mother for the word she needs, she's willing to continue in Portuguese thereafter. I think my wife didn't expect that she'd have to police Isis's speech, and she tends not to do so, so it's up to me to remind them both of the rule. So, I guess I wish Isis's bilingualism weren't another place for me to be the family's main disciplinarian.'

(Don Davis, Boston)

'I would prefer my kids to speak German back to me all the time. But when we travel to Germany, all children tend to switch to German easily if necessary after a short time (two to five days). . . . I was hoping for a more balanced situation but understand why that cannot be, given the circumstances. I still wish my kids would speak more German with me, but I am happy that my 8-year-old middle child is doing a fair amount of it with me.'

(Andreas Schramm, Minnesota)

'Most people assume that it is easiest to speak your native language, but this is not always so. I conduct my life in Hebrew (except when I am in the classroom, teaching English) and although I may express myself more clearly and in a more sophisticated manner in English, I often find it easier to speak Hebrew. Often, when I am tired, I just don't have the strength to speak English to my children. I know that this is not the way it should be (I believe that a parent should be consistent about the language he/she uses), but it is the truth. I know many English speakers who have never spoken English with their children for this exact reason.'

(Bari Nirenberg, Israel)

Some immigrant parents end up using the majority language to their children because they have monolingual majority language speakers in the house. An immigrant mother who works, for example, as a child-minder will not be able to speak her language freely to her child without making her other charges feel left out. Faced with the choice between saying everything twice and switching to the majority language when the other children are present, it is easy to understand how the majority language can take over.

'Yesterday Freddy was at my sister's house for a couple of hours alone. When I went to pick him up I spoke to him in English in their presence, but it did seem false to me. I wonder if Freddy notices. Similarly, I brought him in to my office last week and in front of the others here spoke to him in English. Naturally, he doesn't really respond to me when I speak to him in English. It's all for the comfort of the others – the politeness factor.'

(Margo Miller, USA)

'Let me say that, at times and in certain situations, it would be impolite to those around us to speak English in public. People might think we're either being snooty or trying to "talk behind their back" to their face. It's a problem at parties sometimes. So you talk Spanish.'

(Harold Ormsby L., Mexico)

'Before I would switch to English so as to not exclude anyone. Now I don't care how they feel. My relationship with my son is most important to me.'

(Dr Edgar Monterroso, USA)

'When we had German guests, however, my husband spoke German to them, but still spoke Dutch to the children, which always annoyed me because I considered it rude, especially as I was always asked to translate. Still, the system worked very well.'

(Gabriele Kahn, Oregon)

'At one stage our son complained when someone used the non-expected language, just as has been reported in the literature. He has now stopped doing this, perhaps because of growing metalinguistic awareness: if he can use two languages, why shouldn't other people?'

(Steve Matthews, Hong Kong)

One language—one location (minority language at home)

Parents with different native languages who are concerned that the minority language will not get enough input if it is heard only from one parent may choose the one language—one location model whereby both parents speak the minority language at home to their children. This method is also usually chosen by families where both parents are native speakers of the minority language. This may mean that children meet the majority language for the first time in the neighbourhood play park or when they start at pre-school or school. Fortunately children are generally very motivated to learn the language they need to communicate, and they usually manage very well when they start meeting monolingual majority language speakers. This model is particularly appropriate where the minority language receives little or no support in the community. In such a case the language will need all the input it can get; even the input from a parent for whom it is not a native language can be valuable. Purists might, however, reject the idea of parents speaking any language other than their native language to their children.

'I am a Chicana [a person of Mexican descent living in the USA]. As such I was raised by monolingual Spanish-speaking parents in Los Angeles. My first contact with English occurred in kindergarten and by first grade no other language was accepted by my teachers. This literally meant that unless I asked to go to the toilet in English, I wasn't allowed to go.'

(Anonymous, USA)

'My husband, although American, loves to speak German, and so we all speak German at home. If we didn't, the children might lose the language altogether because they even speak English to each other now most of the time. I know lots of adults here who came to the country as children and totally lost their first language. I always find it hard to imagine when people tell me, "My parents spoke German at home, but I don't speak it".'

(Gabriele Kahn, Oregon)

'I do understand the concern about wanting the child to speak the kindergarten language (usually majority language) before he enters it. However, I think that at that age (about 2½ or 3, I suppose, as it is here in Belgium), the children are pretty able to pick up that new language, especially for that one, because they will be exposed to it most of the day. Before entering kindergarten, I only spoke Spanish and German. The majority language here is French, so I entered kindergarten in French, without knowing a single word of it. My mother tells me that French reached the level of both other languages in a few months. Now French has become my major language. I would rather have concern for the minority language from the start! It's that language that will have to be defended and improved later on. The exposure to majority language will be such that I wouldn't worry for that before kindergarten! Unfortunately, my wife doesn't speak German, so we can't switch to full German exposure at home. I think I would have done it to increase the German influence in our French environment.'

(Alfred Wiesen, Belgium)

'I have come to the conclusion that there is little or no need to expose children to the majority language in the home. We moved to Japan when our oldest (and at that time only) child, Francis, was about 7 months old. Since my wife's (non-native) English is fluent, we began with a policy of 100 per cent English at home with exceptions for socialisation with Japanese speakers. At the time we reasoned that he would get enough exposure to Japanese outside the home, especially once he started school, so we should emphasise English at home in order to maximise the opportunity to become truly bilingual. Anyway, we were satisfied with our English home until Francis was 3. Then we noticed that he was becoming more shy with neighbourhood playmates. We feared it might be because his Japanese progress was lagging behind that of his peers, so my wife began speaking Japanese to him during the day while I was at work, with everyone switching to English when I was at home. The change in Francis was dramatic. Within a couple of months we felt his Japanese had caught up with that of his monolingual friends and his shyness had eased to what we felt was a more healthy level. However, the pendulum did not stop in the middle but has continued on its arc. Our initial opinion about exposure to Japanese at school has proven correct. Francis speaks excellent native Japanese with a strong Osaka accent (though some Japanese might argue that an Osaka accent is anathema to excellence). Our concern now is that at home he has been showing an increasing preference to speak Japanese and a corresponding reluctance to use English. We recently decided that my wife should try to go back to using English during the day, both to encourage Francis to practise and for the sake of our younger children. In retrospect, I think we may have over-reacted when Francis was 3. We have now seen a little more of all the different "problem" stages that children go through and get over before long without any permanent damage. It also happens that his shy period was just after the birth of our second child, and that can certainly be a little stressful for any older sibling. In conclusion, I would recommend to parents in similar situations to start with the 100 per cent minority language home policy and stick with it, as long as there are opportunities for the children to socialise with majority language peers and decent majority language schools. The children will pick up the majority language just fine. (With us, the jury's still out on the minority language.)'

(David Meyer, Japan)

Even in a home where both parents speak the minority language to the children and to each other, and the children answer the parents in that language, the children may speak the majority language between themselves. While this may be disturbing for the parents and seem to upset the minority language only policy that the parents are trying to implement, there is probably little that can be done about it. The relationship between siblings is private and really nothing to do with the parents.

Whether the parents in a mixed language family choose the one person–one language method or the one location–one language method will depend on how well they speak each other's languages. If they are both fluent in the minority language, then they may decide to use that language at home. If the majority language parent can understand the minority language but does not speak it well enough to use it with the children, or if the parents feel that they should each speak their own language to the children right from the word go, then the one person–one language method should be chosen.

'Artificial' bilingualism

It may seem unfair to monolingual couples that they do not have any natural way to give their children what they perceive to be the 'gift' of two languages. There are, however, families who go to extraordinary lengths to arrange for their children to grow up with two languages. Perhaps the most extreme method is simply to uproot the family and move to another country. This places not only the children but also the parents in a situation where they will be exposed to and need to learn a second language. Many European academics view a year or two spent at an American university not only as a step up their own career ladders, but also as a way to give their children a head start in English (and incidentally improve their own English).

A less drastic method is to let the children attend an international school or kindergarten if such an option is available locally. These schools offer education in all subjects through the medium of a language other than the majority language (often English or French). In some cases these schools are intended for pupils who already speak the language of instruction, but there are some cases where schools offer immersion education for beginners, either as a group or together with children who already know the language. Such schools operate in Canada, for example, where French-speaking children are put in English-speaking environments and vice versa, the aim being to give them two languages (see e.g. Swain and Lapkin 1982), and in bilingual parts of Finland, where Swedish-speaking and Finnish-speaking children are given the chance to learn each other's language. Similarly, 'American' schools and 'English' schools can be found all over Europe, from Nicosia to Stockholm. Students at these schools often do very well indeed.

In multilingual situations, such as the cosmopolitan cities of Geneva or Brussels, parents are faced with many choices regarding their children's linguistic development. Couples working for one of the international organisations which have their headquarters in those cities are often mixed, each speaking their own language; in the cities more than one language is heard all round, and many friends and colleagues speak other languages. The school situation reflects the multilingual nature of the city.

'I live in Brussels and am bilingual Danish–English. My wife is Italian. My kids are growing up quadrilingual Italian, Danish, English, French. And there are huge communities here of similarly mixed/ confusing situations.'

(Ian Bo Andersen, Brussels)

'It is absolutely necessary for the parents to decide which language they feel the child should dominate for their future and that is the language in which s/he (maybe particularly he because it is my impression that little girls are often more verbal than little boys) should be schooled – still of course continuing to communicate with a child in other languages which are natural to the family – because after all the spoken language is much less rich in vocabulary, grammar, etc. than the written language. This was a big decision for many of the multicultural families at the UN because it was becoming increasingly evident that English was the most important language in the world and why deprive a child of learning it as a dominant, rather than a second language, when there was the opportunity to do so?'

(Peggy Orchowski, California)

Another way to create a situation where children might naturally come to be exposed to two languages is to employ a foreign au-pair to look after the children, or to place them with an immigrant child-minder who is a native speaker of the language the parents wish the child to acquire. If this option is not available, some monolingual majority language parents enrol their children for foreign language 'lessons' which are suitable for their age group. These lessons usually teach simple games and songs to the children and may help them to minimise their foreign accent if they eventually start learning the same language at school. Unfortunately these kinds of classes are sometimes held by non-native speakers of the language in question. It is just as easy for young children to acquire, say, French with an English accent as with a native-like pronunciation.

There are some ambitious parents who embark on the mission of giving their children a second language which is neither parent's native language. This can be done either with the one person–one language method, whereby only one of the parents speaks the minority language with the children, or by the one location–one language method if both the parents decide to speak the minority language at home. Parents who decide to give their child two languages in this way are usually very motivated, which is a prerequisite for this kind of venture. George Saunders (1982, 1988) describes how he and his wife raised their children bilingually in German and English in Australia, although they were both English speakers from monolingual backgrounds. They had both studied German and lived in Germany and believed that bilingualism would have a positive effect on their children's lives. By all accounts Saunders and his wife were very successful, and managed to give their children a good level of German. His 1988 book is a very readable account of their experiences. Another way is that exemplified in the following extraordinary account.

'All members of my family shared an LI [first language], Finnish. There was no urgent need for us to become multilingual, but my parents had the original idea that my brother and I should be free of emotional ties to a single culture, so that we could choose where we wanted to live. With this end in mind, they wanted us to learn English. They encouraged me to learn to read Finnish quickly by promising me a wristwatch, which I earned by learning to read by age 5. Then we began studying English, as a family, using a course called "English by the Nature Method" (I think). The course consisted of texts given in conventional spelling and then in IPA [International Phonetic Alphabet] below each line. The texts also came on audiotape. It took us about four years of daily study to finish the course. (In retrospect, I realise this is somewhat unusual, but as a child I didn't know other people didn't go about things this way. As far as I remember, I thought it was fun to learn English.) So, when I was about 9, my parents told us that we were to stop speaking Finnish and use just English at home. I felt very threatened, but my parents assured me that I would not forget how to speak Finnish (they weren't really quite right about that, but oh, well) and I adjusted. We were speaking English in a non-English-speaking environment, with no input from native speakers, except for BBC broadcasts and occasional visits with British friends of the family. As a result, my family developed a home-grown variety of English, which, in retrospect, seems like a very bad idea. However, I came to the USA (at age 19) and was able to pick up native-like pronunciation and pragmatics (people don't necessarily notice that I'm not a native speaker of English) so I guess it turned out OK.'

(Mai Kuha, USA)

Chapter 4

Language development

In the first five years of life the vast majority of children become proficient speakers of their first language. This is a remarkable achievement. Although each child is an individual, and will acquire language at his own pace, there are certain stages that all normally developing children pass through.

The first of these stages is the preparatory stage. During their first year children learn to recognise a number of words. This might not seem much; after all, a dog can recognise a number of words too, but the young child has accomplished a great deal more during her first year. She has moved from being able to distinguish between the sounds of any of the world's languages to being able to ignore differences between sounds that are not used in the language or languages spoken to her. She will also have been training her speech organs by babbling – practising the sounds of language and different kinds of intonation patterns. She has also developed her body language and uses it together with intonation so that those around her are seldom unsure about how she feels or what she wants.

Around the end of the child's first year or the beginning of the second year, he will also have begun to produce a few words. Initially the words are produced in isolation, or together with babble. When a young child's own language production gets going, things move fast. By the end of the second year the child will usually have begun stringing words together and be very good at making her wishes known, even without using words. You can get a long way with gesture and intonation if your listener is interested in what you want to say!

From this stage on there is no stopping. The child's vocabulary expands extremely rapidly and the grammar of the language or languages the child is leaning is fleshed out as the child's language tests the patterns he observes to see how to put words together. Linguists are still arguing about whether children growing up with two languages initially develop one system or two (see Foster-Cohen 1999 for a discussion of this matter).

Children who are born into mixed language or immigrant families have an early language development which is in many ways different from that experienced by those born into monolingual majority language families. In the case of mixed language families, where both languages are used at home, the child's main difficulty is caused by the relatively small amount of input in each language. Where monolingual English babies hear both parents saying the same words to them, as in 'Here's your teddy', 'Where's teddy now?', 'What a nice teddy!', children whose parents speak different languages to them will get less input in each language. If parents do not spend equal amounts of time talking to their children, which is the way things work out in most families, there will be little chance for the children to learn the words of one of the languages. The children are going to have a harder time separating the stream of sound into meaningful chunks of language than if they had only one language, because they will hear the same words being repeated less frequently.

Each object having two names is a source of sorrow to some children. Imagine the disappointment felt by the 1-year old who runs excitedly to her mother saying 'sko, sko!' with her new shoe in her hand only to be told 'Well, actually, mummy says shoe', or even worse 'No, it's a shoe'. Perhaps the best thing to say in these circumstances is 'Yes, there's your shoe!' Obviously, great tact is required to help the child realise what is going on: that there are, in fact, two quite separate systems at work here. What the child says is correct, but inappropriate. These children have a lot more to learn than monolingual children.

Consistency on the part of the parents is very helpful in the early stages, that is each parent using a single language when speaking directly to the child and, if possible, not changing according to who else is present. Families find many ways to accommodate their languages, and generally establish unwritten rules about who speaks which language to whom in which circumstances. There is a lot to be said for the one person–one language method whereby each parent speaks their own language to the child come what may. Then the child can associate the words of each language with the appropriate parent. Another common solution is that the minority language is used in the home, and the majority language used outside. For children under 2 or 3 it may be better for the parents to go on speaking the minority language even outside the home, just to help them organise their languages. The most important thing is to find an arrangement that suits everybody in the family. Children usually manage to adapt to whatever system the adults decide on, and can generally cope even with inconsistency in the long run.

Around the age of 2–3, many children who have been brought up with the one person–one language method will have achieved a level of metalinguistic awareness, i.e. they are able to talk about their languages and say things like 'Mummy says "*dress*", daddy says "*klänning*".' The child at this stage is aware that there are two systems, and will often try to keep the development of vocabulary in step, so that a new word in one language will soon be matched by the corresponding word in the other language. The mother can hold up an object and ask the child, 'What's this?' If the child knows the right word, she will give the word in the mother's language. If the father does the same, he will get the word in his language. Many children at this stage will also answer a question like 'What does daddy say?' from the mother with the word in the father's language (which would not usually be used to the mother).

Example

Elisabeth (2;5) is quite happy with her languages and will say to her mother things like 'Pappa says "*macka*"' when she gets a sandwich. When asked 'What does mamma say?' she will say something like 'Mamma says "*sammich*"'. On one occasion she was asked 'What does Elisabeth say?' and she fell silent, looking totally nonplussed.

The child on this level who has realised that there are two systems used by different people has not really caught on to the notion of her own bilingualism. She sees that her parents each use a different system from her and she from them. Her perception of her parents as monolingual speakers of the language they use to her has not been affected by her having heard her parents use the other language to other people, even to each other.

In families who use the one person–one language way of working, some children take the family's convention of who speaks which language to whom a step further and make it into an unbreakable rule. These children will go out of their way to avoid using a word of the inappropriate language to the 'wrong' parent, and will refuse to answer a question which requires this. They may become upset if spoken to in the 'wrong' language, or may find it very funny, even if they are quite used to hearing the parent speak the language to other people. In fact many children assume that all adults are monolingual and may be either horrified or vastly amused if someone outside the immediate family addresses them in the minority language if they know that person to be a majority language speaker.

Examples

Pat (3;10) attends a monolingual Swedish pre-school. One day, when he was being picked up to go home another child's father said "Bye-bye Pat". Pat started sniggering and broke into peals of laughter.

Leif (4;0) wanted to join in his father's "speaking English" game, but could not bring himself to produce any actual English words when speaking directly to his father. When his dad said "Hello Leif, how are you?" Leif wanted to answer, but could not break the iron rule he himself had set up forbidding the inappropriate language to be used, and so answered his father in gibberish.

Active and passive languages

It is not unusual for children to go through a phase of arguing about what things are called (at about 18 months to 3 years the same time as they start arguing about everything else!). A child who insists that a table is a chair can be told that he is wrong, but a child who insists on saying the Spanish *mesa* instead of *table* to her French mother is not really wrong, but just not using the appropriate language. Sometimes children at this age and right on up will prefer a word in one language for some reason and use only that word in both languages, even when they know the word in the other language. Correcting this kind of inappropriate language use can be an uphill struggle, but it may be necessary, especially if words from the majority language are appearing more and more in a child's minority language speech. Accepting the children's use of these words can be the thin end of the wedge, and before you know what has happened the children may be speaking only the majority language. Our policy has been to make sure we use the word in the appropriate language in our response, in case the child did not know it. If that is not enough we would point out that, for example, 'sommarlov in English is summer holidays'. Of course, many families quite systematically and naturally use certain majority language words when there is no adequate way to express what is meant in the minority language. This is usually when discussing things specific to the society of the country in which the family lives.

In many families where the children do not actively speak the minority language even when it is spoken to them, the father is solely responsible for the child's linguistic development in the minority language. For the reasons mentioned above, this may not work very well, although even a passive knowledge of the father's language is well worth having, and invaluable in communicating with relatives. This kind of passive competence in a language can easily be switched to an active command of the language given favourable circumstances and sufficient motivation, for example, going alone to visit cousins who are monolingual speakers of the child's second (passive) language.

Another set of circumstances which may lead to a passive command of the second language is if the minority language parent uses both the minority and the majority language when addressing the child. This can easily become a habit, particularly if monolingual majority language speaking children are regularly present in the home. The choice is then between (a) saying everything twice, once in each language, (b) speaking only the minority language and letting the majority language children feel left out, or letting the children who know both languages translate for them and (c) speaking only the majority language to all the children. This last solution is often adopted, and can lead to the children answering their minority language parent in the majority language, and eventually becoming reluctant to use the minority language at all.

An additional problem here is that if the minority language parent does not use the minority language in front of majority language speakers, perhaps so that they will not feel left out or that they are the subject of discussion, the child may come to feel that the minority language is inferior and not fit for use in public. This can lead to the child becoming embarrassed if the parent uses this language in public places. If things go so far that the minority language parent feels obliged to speak his or her second language in public and even in private to the child, the parent may seem diminished in the eyes of the child. Rather than being eloquent speakers, able to argue convincingly for the principles they believe in, immigrant parents can become hesitant, clumsy speakers. Bringing up a child, with all that it involves, of singing nursery rhymes and reading aloud, persuading, scolding, coping with teenage rhetoric and tantrums and setting limits, is infinitely more difficult through the medium of a second language than through one's native language. This is also an argument for parents to whom it might not seem quite natural to speak their own, minority, language at all to their child if they have no one else to speak it to.

Due to differences in the amount of stimulation and input the child gets in each language, one or other of the child's languages may be dominant at different times. In families where the minority language is spoken to the child by both parents at home, this will be the first dominant language. If the parents each speak their own language to the child, the mother's language may be dominant initially if she spends most time with the child. If the mother's language is the minority language it will probably be overtaken by the majority language when the child starts pre-school or school, if not before. The minority language may again become dominant if an extended stay (of at least a month) in a country where the minority language is spoken can be arranged.

This transfer to majority language speech at the expense of the minority language often seems to come at around 2½ years of age. This happened in several of the families we interviewed. For some it was the end of the child's active use of the minority language, for others, a trip to a country where the minority language is spoken was enough to turn things around and get the child talking the minority language again. This was our experience with Leif at this age. Some of the families who told us about their situation feel that things might have been better if they had done something different.

'Perhaps I would not have responded to my children when they spoke to me in Spanish, if I had it to do over again, in order to oblige them to use English. Basically I suppose that they have assimilated English and that their passive knowledge can be made active when they decide that they want to use English, for whatever reason.'

(Sean Golden, Barcelona)

'It might have been even better if I had held to some "rule" of always speaking English to them and not Swedish, but in reality I think that would have been difficult to achieve. I have submitted to the reality that Sweden is their native country, they have Swedish friends, Swedish schools, but have always maintained that I am American, not Swedish. Our family rules are a mixture of both cultures, so that when they visit their American relatives they can feel a part of that culture as well.'

(Nancy Holm, Sweden)

'I am disappointed that we could not keep the languages in their life more than we have. All of our close friends are bilingual but different languages. I wish now that my husband and I had made a pact. I studied his language but I am not proficient in Arabic. We even tried to start an Arabic-language school with other Arabic-speaking families but it lasted about three months. I don't really know the answer. If the schools had supported the second language by offering a second language that would have been tremendous. I have my sons signed up for Spanish summer camp. I try. I really want them to be bilingual. Everything could have been better with more support in the community through the school. Also it would have helped if my husband and I spoke the same native language or at least tried to learn it on a deeper level. We both regret not being clearer in our expectations and in which language to commit to.'

(Mother in North Carolina)

Interference and mixing

Children who grow up simultaneously learning two (or more) languages usually go through a phase when they mix languages. At the one word utterance level the words seem to come quite indiscriminately from one or other of the languages. By the two or three word stage, mixing is occurring a lot, giving utterances like 'min book' (my book) or 'jag want some' (I want some) from Elisabeth (2;0 and 2;4) or Pat (4;0) saying 'gör so here' (from Swedish *gör så här* (do this)). This mixing phase gets more or less sorted out with time, and children usually learn to keep the languages separate. This is not, however, always the way it works. Some older children may substitute majority language words for minority ones in a minority language sentence without turning a hair. When pushed, they may in fact know all the words they need, but just say the first ones that come into their head, regardless of which language they belong to.

Example

Leif (9;7): 'I don't want to åka to skolan, how many more veckor is it in the sommarlov?' (I don't want to go to school, how many more weeks are there in the summer holidays?)

At home, where everyone understands both languages, this kind of hotchpotch serves its purpose: the sentence is understood without difficulty. With monolingual English-speaking relatives, no mixing occurs. It is not that the child cannot keep the languages apart, rather that he does not choose to. While purists may despair, it is positive that he at least ostensibly speaks the minority language, English, at all. Leif (9;7) still stuck to his rule of speaking English to his mother, but has given up making the slight effort to recall the English word when the Swedish word comes to mind first. At 7, he would ask for vocabulary items before embarking on a sentence. As a laid-back 9-year-old, he felt that as long as the communication works it does not matter how. At 12 he would still sometimes produce this kind of mixed sentence, although he was able to repeat the sentence, substituting all the Swedish words with English ones on request. It is more difficult to make him aware of the grammatical interference from Swedish.

Interference between the languages can be much more subtle than this kind of word substitution. Nuances of meaning and false friends may cause no end of misunderstanding, as well as amusement for children with two languages. Similarly, in their effort to make sense of the linguistic chaos around them, children with two languages may use direct translation between their languages, assuming that a word which has a certain translation in one context will always have that translation.

Examples

The English word *hat* has a wider meaning than the similar Swedish word *hatt* which means top hat, bowler or lady's hat, while the Swedish *mössa* covers caps and the kind of woolly hats children wear. Children talking in Swedish about their *hattar* cause no end of amusement.

The Swedish word *nos* refers to the muzzle of an animal. Anders (3;4) would use it instead of the correct *näsa* in exclamations such as 'min nos!' when he wanted his nose wiped.

The Swedish word for *snowman* is *snögubbe*, *gingerbread man* is *pepparkaksgubbe*, the *green man* when you cross the road is *grön gubbe*, *the man in the moon* is *gubben i månen*. Leif (3;0) transferred this to all occasions when he wanted to say *man* in Swedish, always using *gubbe* which in fact means 'old man' and is not very polite to say about people within their earshot.

Other kinds of interference between the languages can also be observed. Perhaps the most obvious is foreign accent. The majority language spoken outside the family, at school and everywhere else usually becomes older children's dominant language. Very many children brought up with two languages speak the minority language with an accent. This may come as a surprise or even a shock to some parents (it certainly did to us!): were they not supposed to be able to learn to speak without an accent if they started early enough? This seems in part to depend on the child's linguistic ability, so that children who happen not to be fortunate enough to have an ear for languages may end up with the same kind of foreign accent as any majority language speaker would have in the minority language. In the same way as Leif puts Swedish words into an English sentence, he also puts Swedish sounds into English words. Somehow, perhaps because of the relatively little amount of input in English, he has failed to develop a fully separate phonological system and phonotactics for English. This is something we have also observed in other Swedish–English-speaking children in Sweden. Interestingly, the children's foreign accent seems to be diminishing as they grow older and become more aware of the phonetic differences between the languages. This might be an effect of their English lessons in school. They have, for example, learned to pronounce <th> so that Leif (12;0) and Anders (10;3) corrected Pat (6;5) and Elisabeth (4;10) when they said <f> instead of <th>.

Examples

Leif (8;5): 'I fink so' and Pat (4;0): 'Fank you' (even if the pronunciation of *th* as *f* is not unusual even in monolingual

English-speaking children, it is not a feature of the speech of anyone they hear).

Leif (5;0): 'Wery good!'

Anders (7;8) pronounces the sound sequences <rn>, <rt>, <rd> <rs>, <rds>, etc. as retroflex sounds, something like English <n>, <t>, <d>, <sh>, <dsh> with the tongue tip turned upwards and backwards in accordance with Swedish phonology rules so that *birds* becomes something like *birch*. This is now (at 15;2) still observable on occasion.

The British English variation between 'light' and 'dark' <l> was long missing from Leif's and Anders' speech, so that they pronounced both the <l> in *light* and the <l> in *well* without raising the back of the tongue, but they have developed this distinction as they grew older. Pat and Elisabeth have always been able to produce a dark <l>.

The voiced z-sound at the end of words like *flies* is pronounced as an unvoiced hissing <s>.

Leif (9;5): the Swedish vowels /i:/ and /y/ are confused so that *by* (village) became *bi* (bee) in a school dictation.

Sentence structure can often be affected by transfer from one language to the other, giving howlers such as 'I want not' (Leif (5;3)) for 'I don't want to' which is a word-for-word translation from the Swedish 'Jag vill inte' and conversely 'Jag vill ha ett glas av vatten' (I want a glass of water: Anders (7;5)) where the *av* should not be in the Swedish sentence. The boys are now very aware of these kinds of differences (which are explicitly taught in school English lessons) and correct each other and their younger brother and sister regularly, although they do not speak English together.

Given more exposure to the minority language in the future, when these children begin to travel independently, their early experience and excellent understanding of the spoken language will stand them in good stead and provide a solid basis on which their vocabulary and grammar can be developed. Such children have an extensive passive vocabulary, they are willing and able to communicate with English speakers, and have no difficulty making themselves understood or understanding what is said to them. When they come to learn English at school, they will probably manage reasonably well, which they might not have without the early input. The possible effect on Leif's majority (dominant language) Swedish is potentially more serious, but has by no means reached the stage where he seems non-native.

A feature of all kinds of language learning of this kind, where languages are used only in certain circumstances or to certain people (e.g. English is used only to mother, grandmother and mother's friends and their children, while Swedish is used everywhere else) is that vocabulary in the two languages is learned unevenly. The children may know all sorts of words and phrases in English associated with things they have done with their mother, maybe cooking, gardening, cycling, letter-writing, setting the table or making beds. They may not know the corresponding words in Swedish at all, even if it is their dominant language. By the same token they may never have heard the English words for father-type activities, such as fixing the car, sweeping the floor, playing football or working in the forest.

Children are individuals even if they grow up with two languages. What is true for one child may not be for another. No two children have the same combination of strengths and weaknesses even if they are brought up in the same family. Leif and Anders are a good example of this. Leif's Swedish has been dominant since he started pre-school and his English has not developed to a point where it could be called native-like, although he does have a functional command of English which far exceeds that of his monolingual classmates. Anders was at 7;10 about equally strong in both languages. At 10;3 his Swedish was clearly dominant but his English was good, even if his vocabulary was limited by his reluctance to read English books and a lack of English speakers to interact with. His pronunciation was less accented and he hardly ever used Swedish words in English sentences. At 14;10 he is native-like in both languages. He has much better sentence structure than Leif has ever had in English. He simply has a better ear for languages at this stage, and thus is better equipped to become more monolingual-like in both his languages.

Men and women use language differently; it is often the mother in monolingual families who tries to encourage the children to moderate their language and avoid using slang and non-standard expressions, while the father introduces these expressions, perhaps particularly to his sons. If the mother and father speak different languages, they have no opportunity to balance each other's input to the children. The boys' use of their mother's language (English in the case of the children in the examples) may lack a masculine input, sounding perhaps slightly sissified. Conversely, the girls' Swedish, with no mother's touch to moderate the father's speech, may have a tomboyish tone, such as Elisabeth (2;5): 'Nu ska vi käka' ('Grub's up!' – Literally 'Now we're going to eat', where *käka* is a slang word for eat) which is quite inappropriate from a 2-year-old girl!

> 'Parents should stress the importance of both languages. At first, we assumed that if both us parents talked English at home, the kids would pick up acceptable Chinese outside the home. Later we realised my son was speaking a variety of Mandarin we found crude and unsophisticated. The situation improved greatly when my husband began speaking Mandarin with him at home. Input from both parents in both languages is needed, in my opinion, for kids to pick up the "elaborated" version of a language.'
>
> (Karen Steffen Chung, Taiwan)

The critical period hypothesis

If you learn a single language from infancy, you are said to be a native speaker of that language. As long as you get sufficient input in another language, you might be able to achieve native-speaker competence in that language. Unfortunately, it is difficult to get that much input and practice in more than one language. There are, perhaps, some fortunate individuals who can call themselves balanced bilinguals, and who master two (or more) languages as natives, but it is much more common, even among those who have learnt two languages from infancy, that one language becomes dominant and the other is less than native-like.

An adult who comes to a new country and learns the language spoken in that country as an adult will not usually approach native standard. A motivated and/or talented learner may achieve near-native proficiency in the grammar, vocabulary and semantics of the target language, but only exceptional learners will ever come to sound native as well. Small children are able to learn to speak a second language without any trace of a foreign accent, just as they learned their first language. The reasons for this are not fully understood. One possible explanation is encompassed in the critical age or critical period hypothesis, which states that there is a period in a child's development when language acquisition occurs with very little effort, and that after a certain age, the brain is no longer able to learn language in this way. This is based on early theories concerning brain lateralisation and neural plasticity (Penfield 1965; Lenneberg 1967). There is no general agreement about what age this is, but puberty has been suggested as a likely candidate (Major 1990). The critical period hypothesis is not uncontroversial. It has been suggested that differences between child and adult learning patterns may be due to a number of uncontrollable social and cultural factors (Flege 1987). Thomas Scovel's book *A Time to Speak* (1988) gives an excellent exposition of this topic. Scovel concludes that there is a critical period for pronunciation, but finds no evidence that the critical period hypothesis holds true for other aspects of second language learning. He suggests that there may be sociobiological reasons why accents solidify at puberty. It is at that time that other aspects of the individual's perception of his or her own identity surface, and that it is, therefore, appropriate that individuals are marked as belonging to a particular group just then.

Major (1990) found evidence to suggest that it might not be possible for adults who have acquired only one language during the critical period, and who have later been exposed to a second language, to acquire or maintain native-like proficiency in pronunciation in both languages. This would mean that if they were to achieve native-like proficiency in a second language, it would be at the price of native proficiency in the first language. Alternative scenarios would be the maintenance of native proficiency in the first language while native-like proficiency in the second language is never achieved (this is the most common situation for second language learners), or loss of native proficiency in the first language while never acquiring it in the second language. This is quite common among immigrants who spend many years away from their native countries. They are regarded as foreigners in the country in which they live, and find that they are also regarded as foreigners, or at least as different, in their country of origin, because they have partially lost or modified their first language. This is a difficult situation in which to find oneself and entirely in line with the feeling of being a foreigner both in the new country and the country of origin.

'Several times, when I was in France some people have told me that I had an American accent when I spoke French. But I can't really believe, nor understand this.'

(Stephanie Lysee, USA)

'And expect that, if you become fluent in the L2 [second language], your LI will suffer, unless you have an unusual circumstance with lots of contact to both languages in a lot of domains. Although we think of language transfer as being "bad", it is the most normal thing in the world.'

(Janet Fuller, USA)

'I think I can speak reasonable good and accent-free Dutch even after having been away for more than forty years, but it comes slowly. When in Holland I cannot hang on to Dutch and I automatically (in the heat of ambient conversational speech) [shift] to English.'

(Henry K van Eyken, Quebec)

'I would emphasise that they [immigrants] do not and probably should not sacrifice their LI in order to acquire (and become fluent) in L2. Although they need to be flexible and open to new culture as well as to language, it's possible to add one new language rather than replace it.'

(Aya Matsuda, Indiana)

Chapter 5

The child with two languages

Children who grow up with two languages have a unique chance to acquire them both in a way that is not possible for those who meet their second language later in life. These children have potential access to the riches of two cultures, and may become extraordinarily linguistically and culturally competent adults, with the best of two worlds. These children are especially favoured and privileged. However, the presence of two languages may well give them some trouble at all levels of language learning. Children find themselves in a position where they are exposed to more than one language through no doing of their own. We adults have made the choices: the children have not chosen any part of the experience they are going through. It is, therefore, up to us to make things as easy as possible for them, while helping them to get the maximum benefit from the situation.

Advantages and disadvantages of two languages for the child

For the youngest children, living with two languages is primarily negative. Their initial attempts to analyse the stream of sound flowing over them into meaningful units are hindered by the sheer number of different words they hear. Later they need to learn two words for everything and two systems for putting words together. They also have to understand the system of rules regulating who uses which language to whom and when. Failure to grasp the mechanisms of this system will lead to frustration and failed communication, which must be added to the communication difficulties experienced by any child just beginning to talk.

Example

Our children's Swedish paternal grandmother said of Anders when he was 2, 'I can't understand what he is saying, I think it is English.' In fact it was Swedish, but so unclear that only a parent could interpret it.

Older children also have to work harder if they regularly use two languages. They are required to learn more words (although they may not have as large a vocabulary as monolingual speakers even in their dominant language) and more ways of saying things. They will be expected to achieve literacy in both languages, a task which is daunting enough for some children in a single language. However, children learning two languages with alphabetic writing systems will not have to go through all the steps of learning to read twice. The principles of alphabetic writing are common to all the languages of Europe and many other languages. Even languages like Greek, Arabic and Russian have alphabetic systems, and children who can read in one language can usually transfer their acquired decoding skills to another language, even if the correspondences between letters and sounds are not quite the same in both languages. Children needing to learn to read and write Chinese or Japanese as well as a language with an alphabetic writing system have a harder time.

Acquiring literacy in the minority language can open up a new world of literature and thereby language to the child. No amount of visiting the country where the language is spoken or contact with other speakers can hope to give a child as rich a vocabulary and such a mastery of the nuances of the language as a thorough immersion in its children's literature. In some countries, such as Sweden, some schools offer education in the home language (although recent cutbacks have affected this activity severely), often concentrating on reading and writing. In other countries, for example, England, Saturday schools run by the local minority language community have served the same purpose. If neither of these options is available, it is up to the parents to support their children as best they can either within the family or in co-operation with other families in a similar situation. (See Appendix A for ideas for a parents' workshop.)

There are many advantages for the child who has a reasonable mastery of a second language. In the case of an immigrant family, where both parents come from the same language background, the child will need the minority language to communicate with the parents, assuming that the parents use the minority language, even if the child answers them in the majority language. The majority language is needed for school and social activities, and there is not usually any problem getting children to use it. In the case of the mixed language family, the minority language may not be essential for communication; the parent who speaks that language may have at least some knowledge of the majority language for his or her own needs. In both these types of families, a child who can speak or at least understand the minority language has a channel open for communication not only with the parent or parents who speak the language, but also to grandparents, cousins and family friends and their children.

Some children find that their abilities in a second language give them a sense of pride. This is probably dependent on whether the minority language and its speakers have high or low prestige among other children. English is a particularly favoured language in many countries: young people in many parts of the world learn English and admire English-speaking musicians and actors. This means that a child for whom English is the minority language may be very motivated to speak it well, because of a kind of admiration from peers.

When children who can use both their languages go to visit the country where the minority language is spoken, their hard work and that of their parents are seen to be worthwhile. At best, the children find that they can communicate with those around them. Children with passive skills in the minority language at home may blossom into active speakers when they find themselves surrounded by monolingual speakers of the language.

If parents have encouraged their children by praising their skills in the minority language, which is, of course, a very good thing to do, the children may be devastated to realise that they are not actually indistinguishable from monolingual speakers of the minority language. The possibility also exists that the children are not actually fully aware of the cultural differences between the countries. The children may think they are more bilingual and bicultural than they are. This may not be a problem, and can help a shy child to dare to use the weaker language, so there may be no need to disillusion such children.

Being different

In many countries, talking a language other than the majority language in public places will attract attention. How much attention depends on how accustomed the population is to foreign residents and tourists. Interested strangers may ask questions about the children, whether they are bilingual, where they or the parent come from, and so on. Some may even go so far as to offer unsolicited advice about what the parents are doing wrong. Others may be full of admiration for these children who get a second language 'for free'.

Young children are not usually embarrassed by this kind of interest, although they probably will not want to be the object of attention. At some point children become aware that they have two languages and that this is not usual. Sometimes children in their continuous trial and error striving to make sense of the way of the world will come up with odd theories. Anders (3;0) asked if all Mummies speak English, and was quite fascinated by a male visitor from England; he had assumed that men just do not speak English, at least not to children! By the same token, it can be difficult for a parent used to speaking his or her native language to children to switch to the majority language to speak to the children next door.

Some older children may be unwilling to be seen in public with their minority language speaking parent or parents. They do not want to be made an exhibition of by being spoken to in the minority language, still less would they want to be heard speaking it. Sometimes youngsters have lopsided discussions with their immigrant parent where the parent uses the minority language and the child answers in the majority language. At home, they may or may not all speak the minority language. For such children it might be even worse if their parent spoke the majority language in public, especially if his or her command of the language is less than perfect.

Example

An American musician living in Sweden gives occasional concerts. Sometimes his children are in the audience, but they dread him pointing them out to the audience or addressing them directly from the stage because of his strong American accent and poor Swedish.

At a certain age many youngsters find a reason to be ashamed of their parents, even if they do not have another language or come from another country. They may be too rich or too poor or too ugly or too famous or have the wrong car or the wrong clothes or whatever! Most children do not want to stick out in the crowd, and prefer parents who are exactly like everyone else's.

'My family emigrated to the USA when I was a child, and I grew up there, but always conscious of being different from the neighbours' children, who commented on my parents' accents, for instance, or because my parents didn't understand American sports, or care about them, and because my parents' social circle was almost entirely restricted to fellow Irish immigrants, most of whom were Irish speakers from Dingle or Connemara.'

(Sean Golden, Barcelona)

'I acquired Spanish in my childhood, and I didn't understand that my parents, as adult learners, faced a more difficult task. They were trying to learn a language just by interacting with native speakers, without any formal training or any materials besides a pocket dictionary, but I didn't think of that. I honestly thought there was something wrong with them. Not my father, actually; my perception back then was that he wasn't really trying. He would, for instance, resort to the reasonable strategy of using one or two verb forms in all situations, even when they didn't fit. My mother, on the other hand, seemed to be trying very hard; I couldn't understand how she seemingly "forgot" how to pronounce a word right after I told her how.'

(Mai Kuha, USA)

'Our children used to say that I should not speak Spanish as my accent sounds like a Cuban and would get embarrassed when I would speak!'

(R. Chandler-Burns, Mexico)

Bringing home friends

From pre-school right up until they leave home, most children want to bring home their friends from time to time. Generally, the friends are likely to be majority language speakers. Depending on how the family language system works, this may or may not be a problem. Obviously, everything said to visiting children must be in the majority language unless the minority language happens to be a school language, in which case the visitors (if they are good enough in the school language) might be expected to be able to handle (and benefit from) conversation in the minority language, even if they answer in the majority language.

> 'Recently, some of our younger son's friends have asked us to deliberately speak English in front of them, so they'll get a feeling for what the language really sounds like (as opposed to their English teachers' non-use of the language). No problem. Interesting, though. It would be nice to know if these kids' attitude towards bilingualism changed because of this experience; we never will.'
>
> (Harold Ormsby L., Mexico)

If the family system involves speaking the minority language exclusively to the children, perhaps everything can be translated for the benefit of the visitor, or, especially for older children, an exception can be made and everyone can go over to the majority language while the visitor is there. The same applies with an adult visitor, except that an adult visitor might not feel the same pressing need to know exactly what is being said to the children. There is a risk that visitors might feel left out of minority language conversations, or even that remarks about them are being made in the minority language.

Some children might not have prepared their friends for the linguistic scene at home. It could be difficult for them to explain to classmates that they are not the monolinguals they appear to be. Children who grow up with two languages probably take it for granted and may not realise that others may find the situation odd or difficult. While they may not try to keep their bilingual background a secret, they might not actually talk about it.

> 'At nursery school he is very popular. Mothers of other children try to get Peter to make friends with their child, probably in hopes that their child will get early experience with English and foreign culture.'
>
> (John Moore, Japan)

Day-care and school

For children who use only the minority language at home, the first extended encounter with the majority language comes when they start to play with neighbouring children or when they go to day-care or pre-school. Provided that they get enough contact with native speakers of the majority language at pre-school, their acquisition of the majority language is usually rapid. They are of course extraordinarily motivated to find a channel for communication. Problems may arise if minority language speaking children rarely meet native speakers of the majority language, as may happen in areas with large immigrant populations.

Older children who move with their families to a new country may have greater problems. This is especially true if they have started school. They may lose a year or more of schooling before their majority language skills are good enough to let them follow the curriculum work. By that time, they may have fallen behind children their own age. Younger children seem to have fewer problems.

> 'Before my first son went to the USA, he was fluent in French and he could understand everything in English but would never produce any utterance more than one or two words in English. After his first month in the USA, in kindergarten, he spoke perfectly.'
>
> (Gregory Grefenstette, France)
>
> 'When I left my daughter in the classroom that first day she whispered "Mommy, why are they all speaking Spanish?" – we had come from California – and I whispered back as I rushed out the doors "It's French". So that's how much French she knew. . . . By spring she was "fluent".'
>
> (Peggy Orchowski, USA)

For younger children, who are away from home for the first time at day-care or pre-school, parents may notice that the children lack words in the home language to tell about their day's activities. There are often many gaps in these children's vocabulary, not only in the home language, but also in the majority language. If both parents speak the minority language at home, the child may not know words for events and things at home in the school language. In some municipalities in Sweden pre-school children are offered home language training (if large enough groups can be arranged) for the specific purpose of helping the children to do pre-school things in the minority language, to give them the vocabulary and structures to let them talk about pre-school in the home language.

'I started thinking about my wife's experiences as an assistant in a kindergarten. She says that the kids that are the most "uncomfortable" starting in kindergarten are the kids who have only been exposed to a minority language, and no Norwegian. This of course (like everything else) varies a lot from child to child, but children who are already in a difficult situation aren't exactly helped by the fact that they don't understand a word that is said by either the adults or the other kids. To me, this is obvious, but many parents seem to be very eager to get their children to talk the minority language as early as possible, without regard to the fact that the language that the child will be using on a daily basis is neglected. After all, to most people, the mother tongue is the most important, so also for children. My opinion is that the language the child will be using on a daily basis with other people should be the most important to start with. Of course, as soon as the child is "up and running" on the main language, or gets "other help" (teachers, other children) with the majority, the focus could very well be switched to the minority language ... and: Most important: don't let your expectations of having a bilingual child make life more difficult than necessary for your children (note the "more than *necessary*").'

(Roar Pettersen, Norway)

'As Isis has developed interests separate from her activities with her mother, she has learned a lot of English vocabulary for which she lacks the Portuguese equivalents. This makes it very hard for Isis to express herself in Portuguese sometimes, and she tends to give up on saying something to her mother, if she lacks more than a single word for whatever she's trying to talk about. For this reason, my wife has tried to read more Portuguese bedtime stories to her, just as a way of exposing her to more words that she needs to know.'

(Don Davis, Boston)

If the minority language is a school language

If your child's second language is a compulsory school language there are many things to think about. In the case of English in Sweden (and in many other countries) children start to learn English in first, second or third grade (aged 7–9). Initially they learn only words. Gradually the amount of English teaching each week is increased, until, by the age of 16, they are supposed to have a fair command of written and spoken English. Children who speak English at home with one or both parents will naturally get very little out of this teaching. The first vocabulary learning and sentence construction exercises will be far too easy. The teacher is then faced with the problem of pupils who (a) are bored, (b) know all the answers, and (c) either want to show off their knowledge or cringe in embarrassment if the teacher draws attention to their situation. The teacher may at that point appoint the children as assistant teachers, or give them work of their own to do, which is infinitely preferable. The problem is that children who have been living and breathing English all their lives desperately need help with the language, just as monolingual children do, but they require mother tongue education, not foreign language teaching. A sensitive teacher might be able to arrange suitable work for such a child if proper home language teaching by a native speaker is not available.

Since most school teachers are native speakers of the majority language, their skills in the foreign language are unlikely to be perfect. What is a child to do if he feels the teacher to be wrong about some point of language she is teaching? If the child corrects the teacher, the teacher will be embarrassed. The child may not even be correct: his mastery of the second language is probably far from perfect. If the teacher corrects the child, he may be affronted in his capacity as a kind of native speaker. The child's second language is often modelled on a single speaker, the parent, who may speak a different dialect from the standard dialect learned as a foreign language by the teacher. Most importantly, children's time should not be wasted by obliging them to sit through instruction which is patently unsuitable for them. Children with two languages have special needs if they are to reach their full potential in both their languages.

Our own experience of having children learning English at school with their monolingual classmates is mixed. The teaching has been useful in pointing out differences between English and Swedish sentence structure. One problem has been pronunciation. Many of the teachers and education students we have encountered in schools and at the

English Department at Stockholm University (where many take the obligatory English component in teacher training) have strong Swedish accents. Naturally they pass their Swedish accent on to their pupils – the younger the pupils, the closer the approximation to the teacher's pronunciation. When we pointed out a mispronunciation to one of our children, his reaction was that he preferred to pronounce the word like the teacher.

Another problem has been that a child may feel they know better than the teacher but in fact the teacher is right. We have had discussions with one of our children's teachers asking us to point out to the child that the teacher may be right sometimes, and even having us go through a point of grammar in the book with the child, to convince him that we agree with the teacher on this one.

'They [my children] speak Spanish with a Catalan accent. They have no accent in Catalan. They speak English with a Spanish/Catalan accent at times, other times without. They study English in school, since their third year of primary school, which is worse, because they adapt themselves to the pronunciation and grammar of the teacher and/or their fellow students, who are in every case non-native. They don't want to be conspicuous or act as native informants, although everyone expects them to be fluent in English.'

(Sean Golden, Barcelona)

'My son keeps a low profile in English class. His spoken English is much better than the teacher's, but he has learned grammar and spelling at school. In general he seems bored in English class, and gets annoyed at mistakes in the texts and tests, but since he has such a heavy class load, and must now prepare for a difficult senior high school entrance exam, he is glad to have an easy subject.'

(Karen Steffen Chung, Taiwan)

'Knowing Spanish came in handy during my junior high and high school days when I elected to enrol in Spanish classes so that I could get an "easy" A.'

(Anonymous, USA)

'Have a discussion with the teacher and tell her about your home life, the level of English proficiency, and find the right level of English training so that the kids don't get bored with the class.'

(Nancy Holm, Sweden)

'I speak German fluently (although apparently with an English intonation pattern), but my written German is less advanced. I took a couple of German courses in university, but because I learned German as a spoken language, rather than "academically", I found it difficult to understand the grammatical methods used to explain the concepts which I was having difficulty with.'

(Michele Disser, Canada)

Literacy

In some schools in some countries, home language education is offered to children with two languages. In most places no such provision is made, and it is up to the local minority language community (if there is such a thing) or the parents if the children are to become biliterate. Many parents wonder if they should try to teach their children to read in the minority language before they start school, where they will learn to read in the majority language. Unless the parent is knowledgeable about reading techniques, or is willing to study methods for teaching children to read, it will be easier to wait until the child can read in the majority language before going to the weaker language. As we have seen, children whose two languages use alphabetic writing systems can apply the principles of decoding writing that they learn for one language to the other language.

However, children are individuals, and some children just cannot wait to start reading. If you feel you would like to try, then the minority language is probably a good place to start. We have tried showing flashcards to all our 2–3-year-olds with mixed results: Leif learned to recognise about 30 words, but did not really enjoy the exercise. He is still not a keen reader in either language. Anders was completely uninterested, but learned to read by himself, first Swedish then English when he was 5 (school starts at age 7 in Sweden). At 7 he began to read Swedish for pleasure and at about 10;10 he discovered Harry Potter which started him off reading in English. Pat loved the flashcard method and could read simple English and Swedish texts fluently before he was 4. We stopped teaching him at all when he knew 200 words by sight and he worked out phonics in both languages from there by himself. Elisabeth was not at all interested in flashcards, but by 4;10 she was able to read simple words in both languages. Now at 9;5 she enjoys reading in both languages. The point we want to make is that all children are different. Learning to read a second language is not all that difficult if a child can already read one (provided both languages use alphabetic scripts). Let the children lead the way: you will know when they are ready.

Many children are not ready to learn to read until they start school. The school setting provides an important motivation for learning. Some parents find it difficult to set up any kind of structured learning situation at home. If children cannot read or are reluctant readers, read to them! Reading or being read to is an extremely efficient way to increase a child's vocabulary and familiarity with the written language. A side-effect is the widening of experience offered in books, including a good deal of information about the culture in which the book is set. Parents wishing to teach a child about their minority culture will find contemporary works of fiction set in the country in question very useful.

It might be helpful to structure time for working with each language. Schoolchildren probably have homework, which presumably involves the majority language. Many children want a parent to be with them and take them through their homework. This is particularly valuable for children who do not understand all the teacher's explanations. Either parent can help the children, whatever suits the family best. For many children, particularly those who are not keen on doing their homework at all, a regular homework time can be useful, for example after children's TV, before bed. By the same token, some families may find it helpful to reserve some time each week for working with the minority language, that is reading and writing and doing the kind of work that monolingual children do in their native language. Home schooling or ordinary school materials are probably available either from the country the immigrant parent comes from, or can perhaps be obtained through other sources. Ask your relatives or any teacher you know in the appropriate country. You may also be able to order books through a large local bookshop or via the Internet (see Appendix D).

Bilingual and minority language schooling

In some places it might be possible to place children in classes which are taught partly or entirely in the minority language. In many parts of the world there are international classes or schools which teach through English, or other languages. There may also be bilingual classes where teaching is both in the local language and in English or another language. We have experience of both these school forms in Uppsala. International classes for k–9 and bilingual Swedish/English classes for k–6 are run at an ordinary municipal school in Uppsala.

Anders was in a Swedish class until grade 5 (aged 12). Then he started at the international class in Uppsala along with children from all over the world, many of whom were only in Sweden for a short period and spoke little Swedish. All teaching in this class is in English, with native English speakers as teachers. He is now in year 9 and enjoying school.

When Elisabeth was due to start in the first year of compulsory school at the age of 7, the bilingual class was started at the same school. In this class there was one Swedish-speaking teacher and one English-speaking teacher, both natives of the language they were teaching in. After-school care was organised in cooperation with the International classes, i.e. in English. She is now in year 3 and doing very well. While we would not have considered placing either of them in the international class from an early age, because we feel that would have affected their acquisition of Swedish negatively, the bilingual class was a good alternative. Since we plan to live in Sweden for the foreseeable future, it is very important that the children do actually become advanced users of Swedish, and that is difficult without schooling in Swedish.

Chapter 6

Practical parenting in a bilingual home

Help your child to make the most of the situation

If your child is required to live with two languages, there is a lot you can do to help. Even monolingual children do much better if they get support in their linguistic development at home, for example from parents who read to them when they are small and with them when they are older. Children with two languages have more to learn than monolingual children and are therefore in even greater need of support from their parents. Parents in bilingual families need to be very active and to spend a lot of time talking with their children. Books are an important resource. In the mixed language family, the natural thing would be to have each parent read to and sing and play with their child in their own language. Unfortunately, things do not always go as planned. In many monolingual families, only one of the parents, often the mother, ever reads to the children. In spite of the importance of input in both languages, the same may happen in bilingual families. Many fathers, and mothers too, are reluctant to read to their children. If the father's language is the majority language, this is not too big a problem. If the child goes to pre-school, the teachers usually read a great deal, and can to some extent give the child the input they would otherwise have got from a majority language mother. If the father is responsible for the minority language, his input is harder to replace. In fact it seems, in our experience, that mixed language families are often more successful at giving their children two active languages if the mother speaks the minority language than if the father does.

Home language education and Saturday schools

In some countries, some schools and pre-schools offer special teachers several hours a week for groups of immigrant children or those who have a language other than the majority language at home. In other countries the immigrant communities may organise a Saturday school where a native teacher helps the children with the minority language. This kind of teaching is often aimed at establishing or improving literacy in the minority language. Unfortunately, it is not available to all children. Many children are completely without any kind of support in the community for their minority language. In this case it is up to the parents to help their children and to nurture their linguistic development as well as they are able. Appendix B contains suggestions for supporting a child's minority language with others in play-groups and Saturday schools.

> 'My children were never offered English as a second language in schools, and even if they were, I doubt if I would have let them attend. It might be different if they were from Iran, but American English is all around them anyway, it has always been a status for them at school and among friends to be American (they are both American and Swedish citizens) and they have never felt "outside".'
>
> (Nancy Holm, Sweden)

Use any available resources

Parents need to be creative if they are to help their children to become competent speakers of the minority language. They have to arrange for their children to meet other children and adults who speak the minority language so the children understand that there are others who also use the minority language, that it is not a peculiarity only of the child's family. It is particularly valuable for the child to meet other children who speak the minority language so that the child does not only hear adult language. A child who talks only to adults in the minority language may sound precocious and will miss a large part of the language. Of course, the ideal is for children to regularly meet monolingual speakers of the minority language, so that there is no chance of them slipping into the majority language, and so that they will hear speakers who are free from any trace of interference from the majority language.

> 'I do like to have my children meet other English speakers (both children and adults). I feel that this helps them to understand that speaking English isn't something that only Mommy does.'
>
> (Bari Nirenberg, Israel)

One way to arrange this is to make regular trips with the child to countries where the minority language is spoken. This has many advantages for the child's linguistic and cultural awareness, and will give the child a wider experience of the minority language than any other single strategy. Another way is to have monolingual minority speakers visit the family. Suitable visitors might be grandparents, cousins, friends of the minority language parent (especially if they bring their own children), au-pairs or exchange students.

When other people are not available for the child to speak to, books, videos and satellite TV can be helpful. If the child becomes interested in a particular children's TV programme while visiting the minority language country, it may be possible to buy tapes and videos or books with the same characters. Some children will watch videos of children's programmes over and over again, so that they really come to understand every word that is said, even if they might miss things the first few times. Sometimes children memorise chunks of dialogue from the videos: so much the better! They will learn a lot about the language that monolingual children their age use. Some families may want to introduce a minority language only policy when they buy videos. Some children go through a stage when they want to watch a lot of TV. Parents may feel more comfortable letting small children watch a video than TV, so they know what the child is likely to see. If they are going to spend all that time in front of the TV, then let it be in the minority language!

Networking

There are many advantages to getting to know other families who share your linguistic situation. The children benefit from meeting other children who also speak the minority language, and the parents may find they have a lot in common to talk about. In a large city it may not be all that easy to get to know any other residents who may also have the minority language as native language. The ex-pats in the old days often congregated round the local consulate, but that is not the way things work any more. There may be hundreds of fellow speakers of a language walking round oblivious of one another. Sometimes there may be clubs and societies or informal gatherings which represent different groups, but they do not always broadcast their existence. The local university or college of further education can be a source of information; some foreign language departments are involved in the organisation of, say, local Anglo–Swedish or Greco–Italian (or whatever) friendship associations. The English Society in Uppsala, for example, which is organised by the Department of English at the University of Uppsala, organises all sorts of lectures and activities which are often attended by native speakers of English.

More informal gatherings can be more difficult to locate. English-speaking women, for example, often form such groups in cities across Europe. These are sometimes organised under a larger body, for example American Citizens Abroad, but not always. There is also such a group in Uppsala, with English-speaking women from all over the English-speaking world, which meets about every six weeks with a pot-luck supper in one or other of the members' homes. These groups offer an invaluable source of contacts for new arrivals, if they are fortunate enough to come across someone willing to tell them about it and to invite them to come along to a party, since membership is by invitation only. This kind of group exists in many places, and could be organised by enterprising individuals in many more places.

'The ESW [English-Speaking Women] is located in Helsinki but has members all over Finland. We do have a newsletter. The organisation was very important to me when I first came to Finland, because twenty years ago almost no one in Finland spoke English, the major foreign language was German. Today most of the newly arrived women don't join us because almost everyone under 30 now speaks fairly good English, especially those who are in/went to university. There is another group, International Women's Club, for all foreign women who live in Finland, but it meets during the morning and is primarily for wives who have accompanied husbands who have temp jobs (two-year tours). There is also an American Women's Club, but it also meets during the day and seems to consist primarily of embassy wives and American businessmen's wives. I was very active in the ESW when I was working at home and raising

> the kids, because it was my only contact with English and practically
> my only contact outside the walls of home.'
>
>   (Deborah D. Kela Ruuskanen, Finland)

You may be able to meet fellow native speakers through your religious
meeting place or through a local adult education organisation. You might
be prepared to advertise in the local newspaper, suggesting that fellow
countrymen and women contact you, or maybe meet in a pub one
evening. You might be surprised at the response! Once you meet others
you may be able to arrange activities for the children, such as Saturday
school, toddlers' group, play-school or just occasional outings or picnics.
Practical suggestions for organising this kind of activity will be found in
Appendix B. The following section summarises what we feel to be the
most important ways you can help your child.

Practical advice for parents whose child has two languages

- Speak your own language to your child unless there are compelling
  reasons why another arrangement is preferable.
- Be consistent in your choice of language to a young child. If you
  want to use different languages with your child in different
  situations, stick to the system you devise.
- Travel as often as possible to a country where the minority language
  is spoken. Ideally you should go to the place where the parent
  responsible for that language is from, especially if there are relatives
  there for the child to get to know. It is important for these children to
  realise that their immigrant parent also has a background.
- Meet other children and adults who speak the minority language.
  Ideally these should be monolingual speakers, since otherwise they
  might mix the languages or switch to the majority language.
  Structured activities with other children through the medium of the
  minority language can be very valuable. For children up to 3 or 4, a
  parents and toddlers' group can be a lot of fun for both children and
  adults. For older children, a play-school with a native minority
  language speaking teacher can bring the child's level of language up
  considerably.
- Try to get hold of and use as many age-appropriate language
  materials as possible in the minority language: story books and
  workbooks, tapes, videos, computer games, whatever you and your

children feel comfortable with. In a mixed family, both parents should read, talk and play with the children, each in their own language. A child with two languages needs to work and play more with language than a monolingual child who has two parents giving input in a single language. It is just as important to nurture the majority language, which will presumably be the child's dominant language and the language of schooling eventually. Do not leave the majority language to look after itself. Try and support your child's development in both languages just as you would if each was the only language in the family.

- Try to ensure that your child learns to read, and preferably also to write, in the minority language. Our experience is that this can be done before or after the child starts school in the majority language, depending on the child's readiness and interest.
- For the sake of the child's weaker language, consider an extended stay in a country where it is spoken as the majority language.
- Consider letting teenagers visit the minority language country on their own, to visit cousins or friends or on a summer exchange visit, or to spend a term or a year in school.
- If the family regularly returns to the same place in a country where the minority language is spoken, for example to visit grandparents, cousins or friends, it may be possible to arrange for even quite young children to attend school for a few days or longer. The potential advantages of this are manifold: the children get to know mono-lingual speakers of their own age, they learn to use their weaker language in different situations, they learn about the culture of the country and they are able to compare their own school with something else, giving them a new perspective on their lives at home.

We have, in our own experience, had mixed results with this kind of mini-immersion in the immigrant parent's language and culture, which two of our children tried in consecutive years in a primary school in Northern Ireland. The first year, both children (aged 7 and 5) enjoyed their two days in school enormously, revelling in being at the centre of attention, each surrounded by a crowd of eagerly curious classmates at each break. They were even invited home to tea on the second day: what an experience that was! The next year, the younger child managed well, but the older child came home in floods of tears at the first break. The teacher had been cross, he said. Not actually at him, but the tone was too far removed from the traditionally calm and encouraging tone in Swedish classrooms. And yes, it has to be said, some of the teachers we saw at the school did seem to try to get order by yelling and snapping at the children. The actual level of discipline does not, however, seem to be any different in the two countries. Well, at least he appreciated his own teacher in Sweden more after that!

We have also sent our older children to stay on their own with relatives and friends in England. While they enjoyed themselves enormously, this was much more a cultural experience than a linguistic one. The same is true of having cousins and other English speakers visit us. The children's English is now so well established that this kind of input does little for it, but it is valuable for their sense of background and belonging to meet as many relatives and other English speakers as possible. With younger children, the situation is quite different and any minority-language speaking visitor or time spent in an environment where the minority language is spoken will be immensely valuable for the child's perception of the language.

'In addition to frequent trips home to Minnesota, I read to them most nights, and try to cover things like Greek and Roman myths, Mother Goose, the Bible, science books – things I think that can give them solid, useful background in English and Western culture.'

(Karen Steffen Chung, Taiwan)

'Consistency, from the first day on, is important. We spoke in German, read in German, and had the children listen to a German cassette every evening before going to bed.'

(Thomas Beyer, USA)

'I try to spend some time each night going through some short reading and writing exercises in German with my kids. They like the attention and are therefore rather motivated to learn German even when they are tired.'

(Andreas Schramm, Minnesota)

'We really want our daughter to be a bilingual and we are planning to have regular play-group sessions with other Japanese-speaking children.'

(Kaori Matsuda, Australia)

'One thing I am thinking of and many other Japanese mothers have done is to send the child(ren) to their grandparents'/ auntie's places in Japan during the school holidays. This is very costly but seems to be the most effective way. If she can I want her to go to Japanese school (primary or secondary) for one year.'

(Kaori Matsuda, Australia)

'In my first years in New York I was sent to a Russian Orthodox nursery school where we spoke only Russian. My mother spoke Russian and some German to me at home, while my father spoke only English (he does not speak or understand any foreign languages). When I was 7 my parents moved to Washington, DC and there was no Russian school, so I started in the US public school system. At this time my mother was in close contact with her brother and sister, both of whom usually speak German with her, so we often switched from Russian to German. I was sent to Germany for three months each summer to stay with relatives and my mother concentrated on speaking mostly German with me at home in order to prepare me for those summers. We also practised reading and writing (my mother is a teacher).'

(Ingrid K. Bowman, Hong Kong)

'We have a lot of educational videos. We work with pre-school activities in both languages, alternating nights.'

(American mother in Sweden)

'Because she's home-schooled, she studies her languages formally, a little bit each day. Her favourite is Latin, because her Portuguese makes it easy. . . . Chinese is harder, so she doesn't usually like studying it as much, though she likes using it.'

(Don Davis, Boston)

'I think a very important factor is praise: people tend, more than they should, to take it for granted that Brazilian kids speak Portuguese, and that Chinese kids speak Chinese. Try to remember that being a polyglot is a difficult achievement, and praise the kid accordingly and constantly for his or her efforts.'

(Don Davis, Boston)

Things to do at home

All the above tips show that parents can do a great deal to support all aspects of their child's development. If they are actively involved in what their children are doing they have a better chance of stimulating their development in both their languages. Parents whose children are to acquire two languages do not need to behave any differently from any other parents. The point is that their children are in greater need of active, aware parents who can help them make the most of their languages.

Talk to your child

This may seem obvious, but some parents find they do not actually say all that much to their child, particularly in the first two years before the child has begun to use words to communicate. While small children are extremely good at letting us know what they want even without the use of words, there is no reason for the parent to rely on smiles, gestures and hugs for communication. A chatty parent will be a major resource for the child, letting the child hear a large number of words in many different contexts. A child growing up with two languages has that much more to learn, and needs as much linguistic stimulation as possible in both languages.

Talk to your children about what you are doing, be it changing a nappy or digging the garden. Talk to them about what you will do together later and about what happened yesterday, whether they understand or not. Let the words flow over them. If you talk as though they understand, they will come to understand, and in the meantime they will love the sound of your voice and being with you and having your attention.

If your child is to learn one language from each parent, it may be necessary to ensure that both parents get time to spend with the child. There is often a problem if the parent who is solely responsible for the minority language is not often at home. In many families the father works while the mother is at home with the children, at least while they are small. Even if both parents work, the father may work longer hours than the mother, and may simply not be able to spend enough time with the child. The family may want to take steps to allow the father more time with the children if it is important for them that the children acquire the father's language.

Listen to your child

Communication, even with a tiny baby, is a two-way affair. Given the chance, babies are fully able to take their turn in the conversation, although they may have no words. When you chat to your children, it is important to give them a chance to respond. Ask them questions, and wait for the answer. If you say something like 'Are you hungry then?' to your baby, you will probably get a smile or gurgle in reply. Then you can paraphrase that and expand on it, saying something like 'Yes you are, you're starving, aren't you!' With slightly older children who are starting to talk, you can do the same: wait for their answer and expand on it or fix it up into a grammatical utterance and give it back to them:

Parent: 'Shall we go shopping?'
Child: 'Trolley!'
Parent: 'Yes, you can sit in the trolley, can't you? You like that, don't you?'

The child who is learning two languages needs exactly the same kind of help as the child who is learning only one language, but more of it. In addition, the child may need some help to get the languages sorted out, so that if the child in the above example had said the Swedish word 'Vagn!' instead of 'Trolley!', the parent's answer could have been just the same, although this would also be letting the child know that the appropriate word was *trolley*. This can be done without any kind of overt correction, just as part of the conversation. Even older children's errors in one or other of their languages or the use of the 'wrong' language can be dealt with in this same way, by giving the correct form, expanding on what the child said and inviting the child to go on with the conversation.

Keep track of your children's development

David Crystal's excellent book *Listen to your Child* (1986) has a lot of helpful information for parents who are interested in following the development of their children's language. He suggests that parents keep track of their child's progress by keeping a diary and even making sound recordings. This is not always easy to do, despite the best intentions. Countless professional linguists who start out to document the linguistic development of their own children never actually get very far. Nonetheless, some kind of documentation is interesting and useful to have, especially if you have more than one child, so that you can consult your notes on an older child and see what he or she was saying at the same age as a younger child. The added feature of having two developing languages makes the whole process even more fascinating and provides entertaining reading for children and parents alike in years to come. If you want to record your child, the following points are worth bearing in mind:

- An ordinary radio/cassette recorder will do fine unless you think you are likely to want to get involved with advanced editing. If there is a microphone built into the cassette recorder, that is perfectly adequate for this kind of recording, and more convenient than a separate microphone. Most children are used to seeing a radio/cassette recorder on the table rather than a microphone; one problem with a separate microphone is that small children are often more interested in trying to grab it than in talking.
- Many families have video cameras. The advantages of making a video recording are many. Children are often very used to being filmed. Having pictures means that you can document much more about what is going on around the child. It is easier to put the recording in its context if there are pictures as well as sound, and you can see the child's behaviour as well as hearing speech. Many video cameras have a system for the simple editing of recordings, meaning that a shorter, more interesting film can be made.
- Choose your setting with some care. Ideally, for both sound and video recording, you want to be able to set up the equipment and leave it to look after itself until the recording session is over. We have successfully rigged up the video camera on a high shelf pointing at the kitchen table and recorded whole family mealtimes, from the stressful hungry settling down to the calm sated leaving the table. This can be a good way to make language recordings too. If you want to record one child talking to a parent, try to get any other people out of the room. Provide something for the conversation to be based on: a book, some toys, play-dough or whatever you think might work for your child.
- In a mixed language family you will need to have both parents separately interacting with the child, each in their own language. If both parents speak the minority language at home, you may have to invite someone the child knows in the majority language to come and talk to the child, or take the equipment along on a visit to such a person. You may want to make the settings as similar as possible in both languages, and have, say, the child playing with the same toys with both parents in turn, each in their own language.

- On other occasions you might want to document the child's use of language with a brother or sister or visiting friends, or even show how the whole family's interaction is with frequent language switching and mixing. Then the use of a video camera which is rigged up to film, say, the area round a table can be a great way to get really spontaneous speech. If you are not a part of the conversation you want to record, you will need to provide something for the children to do which will keep them at the table for a while, preferably something that is not too noisy. They will soon forget about the camera, particularly if you leave the room and let them get on with it.

- It is helpful to have a regular time and place to make recordings, so that they are less likely to be forgotten. The first weekend in each month might be about right. You do not need to record for very long each time.

You might like to keep a written record of your child's development. Appendix C has pages that can be copied and used to make notes about your child's progress. If you make notes every six months, then you are likely to see considerable development each time.

Read to your child

All the experts are agreed that regularly reading to young children is a superb way to stimulate their language. Teachers of young children claim to be able to tell which children in their class are read to at home. For a child with two languages, being read to becomes even more important. If children have a limited vocabulary, it is easy for parents to use only words they know their children understand when talking to them, meaning that the children do not often get a chance to learn a new word. Reading books to children opens new worlds to them. If there are many unfamiliar words in the text, you may want to substitute some of them with words the children know, but an alternative is to use the word and explain it straight away. Try to follow up the reading in some way; maybe you can use the new words in speaking to the children, asking if they remember what the word was. Children with two languages may need books intended for somewhat younger children in their weaker language.

'I read stories to them in English, at bedtime, and this has shown how limited their vocabulary is. That is, I have almost unconsciously limited the lexicon I use with them, and when I read a children's book to them there are many words, grammatical structures, and cultural references they do not understand. . . . When I read to them in English now, I make more of an effort to stick to the authentic English vocabulary and syntax, though this means they will miss many details. Sometimes they ask for explanations. More often I slip them in while reading to them.'

(Sean Golden, Barcelona)

In a mixed language family who use the one person–one language method with their children, the minority language needs more support than the majority language. The child will be read to in the majority language at school. Nonetheless, being read to is important for both languages. A reasonable compromise might be that the majority parent reads the bedtime story at the weekend and the minority language parent on week-nights. Of course, this will not work in all families, but it might be worth aiming at. Do not stop reading to your children just because they have learned to read. It may be a long time before their reading is fluent enough to let them concentrate on the story rather than on the reading. You can read them stories that will stretch their language, but that would be too difficult for them to read themselves. One of our children found audiobooks in English very useful before her reading skills in English were up to reading the level of book she was ready for intellectually.

Teach your child to read in the minority language

A child who can read is in a position to go on alone into the world of children's literature. Most parents want their children to be literate in both their languages. If home language education is not offered at school or the minority language is not a school subject, you as a parent will have to help. Even if there is help available from school, parents need to ask themselves which language they want their children to read first. In the case of two writing systems which use the same alphabet, there is not much difficulty in learning to read the second language. If the alphabets are different (for example, English, Arabic, Greek, Russian) or a whole different writing system is involved (for example, Chinese, Japanese) there are more problems.

If you want to teach your children to read the minority language at home before they start school, we recommend two books to help you get going. Glenn Doman's *How to Teach your Baby to Read* (1975) uses flashcards to teach children to sight-read initially after which they are ready to work out the correspondence between sound and letters on their own. While Doman recommends his method for young babies, we found it to work well for one of our children from around 2 years; our other children were not interested. This kind of reading may not have much value until the children are old enough to understand the words they are reading, but it is a lovely game to play if the child is interested. Peter Young and Colin Tyre's holistic model of reading where reading, writing and spelling go hand in hand is described in their book *Teach your Child to Read* (1985). Whether or not your child actually learns to read before starting school, just the contact and communication between you and your child which the attempt to learn to read involves make it worthwhile.

If you decide to wait with the minority language until after the child has learned to read the majority language, the process may be easier for many children. Having mastered reading in one language, they will often be able to pick it up very quickly in the other language, often without much in the way of formal teaching, just by following the text when they are being read to. The problem then may be to motivate them to read in the minority language, when they find it easier in the majority language.

In our experience, children may be reluctant to read in the minority language even after they are technically able to do so. They may find that they are not able to read books at their age level, and that the books they can read are not of interest to them. Our solution has been to let the children listen to a taped reading of the book while they follow the text in the printed book. This has been successful, although the taped readings are not easy to obtain. You may need to find some way to motivate children to read in the minority language, such as some kind of reward system. We found that time on the Internet was a strong motivator for our oldest children at about 10-12 years of age, with fifteen minutes' reading (or reading/listening) giving the right to fifteen minutes' Internet time. Other children will, of course, find other rewards worth reading for. With all four of our children we have summer holiday reading schemes, where pages count for points and the target (they pool points for this) is a trip to the Gröna Lund fairground in Stockholm, with various minor rewards along the way.

The point of all this pushing and persuasion is of course to get the children to read enough to discover that reading has its own rewards. When a child becomes an independent reader there is no limit to the amount of vocabulary and language that will be acquired. Extensive reading for pleasure is one of the most efficient ways to develop language both for native and non-native speakers of any age.

Obtain material in the minority language

Other media are also valuable for children. At a certain age, many children want to do nothing but watch their favourite video tapes over and over again. You might like to enforce a minority language only policy for videos. Even if video-watching is generally of limited value, a 4-year-old who watches, for example, *Postman Pat* or *Sesame Street ABC* for the umpteenth time is learning English in a way he never could if he saw the programme only once, he is learning a lot about the culture of Britain or the USA, he is getting the same kind of children's culture as his peers in English-speaking countries and if his English-speaking parent sits in just once, they have the makings of countless conversations. In such a case, it can be invaluable to follow up the child's video encounters with *Postman Pat* or *Sesame Street* books, tapes and even non-linguistic props, such as pillowcases or backpacks. If a child is into computer games, try to steer her towards educational games in the minority language, particularly those which train language.

Many parents ask relatives in the minority language's country to send books, tapes and videos rather than toys or clothes when buying presents for the child. It can sometimes be difficult to get hold of materials from abroad. If you have the opportunity to travel to your 'home country' you can search the bookshops for suitable material. We generally travel to Ireland with two empty suitcases, one nested inside the other. They are full of books and videos when we get back to Sweden.

For some minority languages it may be possible to buy books, tapes and other material by mail order, even via the Internet. Ask around: the Internet mailing list Biling-Fam is a valuable source of information, and you can use a search engine to find other Internet resources (see Appendix D). Multilingual Matters' *Bilingual Family Newsletter* is full of information and tips from other parents. (To subscribe, write to Multilingual Matters, Subscriptions, Frankfurt Lodge, Clevedon Hall, Victoria Road, Clevedon, Avon, UK, BS21 7SJ.)

Chapter 7

Competence in two cultures

Access to two cultures

Children can be brought up with two languages in any number of different ways. Whether parents have decided that their child should learn a language which neither of them speak as natives, or whether one or both of them have a minority language which they want to share with their child, they will have to make decisions concerning the culture or cultures which are associated with the language. Knowing a language without being familiar with an associated culture is an academic skill which, while it is valuable in itself, is not always what parents raising their children with two languages had in mind.

Language is often the least of the problems facing a mixed language family. The cultural differences between the parents will often be far more significant. Even where the two cultures involved are ostensibly not far removed from each other, as is the case in the countries of northern Europe or southern Europe, the differences can create major difficulties. For example, the Irish and Swedish ways of doing things may seem to be superficially more similar than different: both countries have Christian traditions, both are agricultural, both have violins and accordions in their folk music, both consume a lot of potatoes, carrots and swedes. Nonetheless, there are thousands of small differences and peculiarities on either side that can lead to misunderstanding and confusion, as well as much amusement. In fact, it is much easier to make allowances for the big differences. It is the small unexpected things that cause problems. Let us take a look at some areas where cultural differences can become important to a family.

Should children brought up bilingually also become bicultural?

The decision to bring up children so that they are familiar with two cultures is not as straightforward as the decision to let them acquire two languages from their parents or others outside or within the home. Children can acquire a language simply by having it spoken to them and being in a situation where they are motivated to use the language for communication. It is far more difficult to arrange for children to acquire knowledge of a culture in the same uncontrived way. While parents alone can give children a second language, they will not be able to give them a second culture without the help of others and the support of society. It is not impossible for a child to acquire knowledge of two cultures, but it requires some work on the part of the parents.

Some families may choose not even to attempt to make their children familiar with the culture associated with the language they speak. Immigrant parents who have become integrated into the majority society may feel no need to pass on the culture they grew up with to their children. The practical difficulties involved may be just too great, especially if the family has little or no contact with others who share the immigrant parent's background. Some immigrant parents may feel that their children need to be fully integrated into the majority society and that any attempt to keep up the ways of the country of origin or to pass on that culture to the children would not be in their interests. Other families have a great need for the children to become familiar with the ways of the 'old country', perhaps for religious reasons.

For families where both parents have a common minority background, the situation is somewhat easier. The minority culture does not have as much competition from the majority culture in the home. Nonetheless, children have contact with the society in which they live through school, friends, sports and other activities. This means that this competition grows as the children get older and become more involved with the world outside the family.

In the case of families where neither parent is a native speaker of the minority language, it is more difficult to familiarise the children with the culture of a country where the language is spoken. Where a minority language or mixed language family can keep the traditions of the minority culture and pass on that culture's ways of looking at the world, any attempt by a majority language family to teach the children the customs of the culture associated with the minority language that one or both of them has chosen to speak with the children may seem contrived. In such a case, it is probably better to rely on frequent trips to a country where the minority language is spoken.

Parents who want to let their children become familiar with the culture associated with their second (minority) language should think long and hard about how best to go about it, just as they need to do when working out how best to support their children's linguistic development. If the ambition is to let the child later feel as though they are equally at home in two countries, more will be required than if the child is only to know how to be polite in the minority parent's country. Either way, the parents can do a great deal at home to prepare the child for visits to the other country.

Feeling at home

Children going to visit, say, grandparents in another country may be very disappointed if they find that there is a lot going on around them which is quite incomprehensible. Even if they have learned their grandparents' language reasonably well and can communicate without too many misunderstandings, they may find that they feel very different from children their own age in their grandparents' country. They might have expected to feel like more than visitors. Parents might expect their children to know intuitively how to behave, as though they should have soaked up such things along with the minority language at home. Mixed language families usually teach their children primarily the manners of the country in which they live. It is questionable whether it is feasible to teach young children two sets of ways to behave. Switching cultural codes is not as easy as switching languages.

An adult brought up with two languages might feel the lack of facility in the culture of the second language even more acutely. It is a sad thing to visit the country in which your mother was brought up and feel like a foreigner. Many families want to avoid their children feeling like foreigners or being perceived by others as foreign in either the country in which they live or the home country of one or both parents. Others may feel that this is not really important. Each family needs to make their own decision, but let it be an active decision. Left to themselves, children are unlikely to acquire any culture other than that in which they live and go to school. If they are to feel at home somewhere else as well, it requires an effort by their parents. Some parts of any culture are best learned by children, for example children's books and games which are part of the common background of those who know the culture from the inside. These cannot be learned later instead. Childhood memories are an important part of being a native of a culture. There is much the parent can do to help the child in this respect.

Practice makes perfect. It is unrealistic to think that children can be so well prepared with knowledge about their second culture at home in one country that they will feel immediately at home in another country. The best way to become familiar with the culture of a country is to be in that country as much as possible. From the point of view of acquiring the cultural competence needed to be at home in two cultures, the ideal would be to spend half the year in each country. This would also be an excellent way to learn both languages. However, this is not the way most families choose to live, and such an unsettled way of life would have many other disadvantages, especially for children. But frequent visits to the minority language's country and meeting many different people there, especially other children and their families, will teach the children who live elsewhere much about the way of life. Perhaps they can visit their cousins or their parents' friends if they have children around the same age.

'German, Dutch, and English are closely related so that a real "culture shock" doesn't occur (well, unless you move to America ...).'

(Gabriele Kahn, Oregon)

'I make an effort to expose her to other Japanese people around us. Luckily I know some Japanese families [both parents are Japanese] and they often invite me and my daughter to their place. This gives her opportunity to understand Japanese culture.'

(Kaori Matsuda, Australia)

'Knowing about the culture builds memories and makes the concepts/words of the minority language come alive and real.'

(Andreas Schramm, Minnesota)

Knowing how to behave

Children who grow up in a country learn a great deal about that country's way of life through their own observations, doing as others do, doing what adults tell them, listening to the conversation of adults, watching television and attending school. If children who live in another country come to visit, they may not be aware of the background to what they see around them. If, for example, a child from another country visits Northern Ireland, bombed-out shop-fronts and road-blocks where armed soldiers point machine guns at cars will probably seem very alarming. Children who visit Sweden may be puzzled by the way people take their shoes off when they go into people's homes, and even certain kinds of public places, such as children's clinics or nursery schools. Children who visit Spain from other countries may be disconcerted when adults they do not know talk to them. Children who visit England may wonder why they are often ignored by adults. Every country has its peculiarities.

Preparing a child for a trip to the minority language country is not easy. Parents will probably want people they visit to think that their children are well brought up. The problem is that being well brought up means different things in different cultures. It is, of course, most important that the children behave appropriately in the country in which they actually live. While at home, the norms of the majority culture may be applied, but the immigrant parent may feel under great pressure to behave according to his or her native culture while visiting the country of origin. This might mean being a lot more strict with the children than normal, which can be very confusing for the children.

We experienced this several times when we (with two children) were visiting friends in England who also had two children. The children were getting along very well together, if a bit rowdily. Our friends kept hushing their children, obliging us to do the same, although the noise level was a lot less than would usually have been tolerated according to Swedish standards of behaviour.

Religion

Religion and culture are intimately associated with each other. Even in cases when both members of a couple appear to have the same religion, i.e. if they are both Roman Catholics, or both agnostic, or both Protestant, there can be vast differences between the way they view things. A Polish Catholic does not have the same kind of religious life as a French Catholic, nor is a Swedish Lutheran the same as an English Anglican. National characteristics influence the way religion is applied to everyday life. Some societies are more secularised than others.

Religion is not always quite as loaded as it is in Northern Ireland or Bosnia Herzegovina, say, but can nonetheless cause trouble to couples in international relationships. Questions such as whether and where to get married can be problematic; couples may decide not to get married at all. In some countries living together before getting married is not viewed as appropriate. Many parents have breathed a sigh of relief when their children decide to get married, whether it is to a 'foreigner' or not.

Getting married in a church can be difficult if more than one religion is involved. The couple may have to promise to raise any children in one of their religions before they can get married. There may even be pressure put on one of the couple to convert to the other's religion. Even if neither of them is religious, they may experience pressure on them to get married in church. For many people, even those who are not religious, a church wedding is seen as a part of tradition, and a civil ceremony seems like a not very adequate second best. The same is true of baptising children. For some (for example, Roman Catholics) baptism is seen as a formal entrance into the Church; for others (for example, many Swedes) baptism is thought of as a traditional naming ceremony with minimal religious significance. A conscious decision not to baptise one's children in Sweden is viewed with utter bafflement by many. In a family where the parents come from different religious traditions the religious upbringing of the children will need to be discussed, particularly if the parents are active in a congregation.

Achieving cultural competence

Children with two languages are often highly motivated to learn appropriate behaviour when they visit the country where the minority language is spoken. They want to fit in and be like everybody else, particularly when they are with other children. They may also be willing to learn new patterns of behaviour to earn the approval of grandparents and other adults.

Example

Leif (8;6) to his grandmother in Ireland: 'In Sweden we say "tack för maten" to pappa and "thank you for the food" to mamma, but we can say "please may I leave the table" to you.'

No method of teaching children about the culture of their parent's homeland can ever be as effective as actually taking them there to see for themselves. If the family's ambition is to have the children able to operate like natives of both the languages and cultures involved in their lives, without ever feeling like foreigners, there is a lot they need to learn. This level of competence might never actually be attained, at least not during childhood. This learning process can, however, be begun at home, with the minority language parent telling the children about life in the other country, and making the trappings of childhood in the other country available to the children. Bear in mind that the parent may not be all that well informed about recent developments and changes in society, and may know very little about current trends in child-rearing in the home country. Visitors from the country where the minority language is spoken can be a valuable resource for the children. Unfortunately such visitors are often not aware of the family's situation, and may even insist on speaking the majority language to the children. Let us consider some features of what the potentially bicultural child needs to know.

Social behaviour

People in different countries have diverse norms of behaviour. While there are differences between individuals and families, each culture has its own ways. There are all sorts of cultural variations, for example in the way people greet each other and children (kiss, embrace, shake hands, make eye-contact, nod, say hello, etc.). They expect different behaviour from children too. Some cultures are much more tolerant of children than others. Problems with this can arise in bicultural families. Even details like how often eye-contact is made and how long it is held vary between cultures. Failure to make eye-contact as often as expected can give an impression of shiftiness, while overdoing it can be very off-putting for the other. How loudly and how much a person should speak vary in different cultures, as does how close people stand to each other when talking.

Being polite is another potential area of difficulty for those who need to operate adequately in two cultures. Words like 'please' and 'thank you' do not exist in all languages, and where they do exist, they will probably not be used the same way. The German word *bitte* sometimes means 'please' and sometimes not. The Swedish word *tack* can mean 'please' or 'thank you', depending on the context. These words are, however, very important, and taking the time to teach their correct use to the children will do a lot to improve their perceived politeness in the other country. A failure to say 'please' in the English-speaking world can make a child or adult look very rude or foreign in some circumstances. Taxi-drivers and ticket collectors can be scathing to any hapless foreigner who forgets to say 'please' and 'thank you'.

Religion is an important part of many cultures. Children cannot reasonably be given two religions, but they do need to be aware of the differences between the religion of the 'second' culture as well as the religion of their primary culture. A family where both parents are immigrants from the same place may share the same cultural background and religion and naturally pass it on to their children, even if they live in a country where the majority have a different religion. A mixed couple may have settled for one or the other's religion, or simply not be religious. Religion can be a sensitive matter for grandparents on both sides of the mixed language/culture family. Whatever solution the family comes up with, they risk offending religious sensibilities on one or other side of the family.

'Our situation is complicated by the fact that we're Jews; however, the problems that derive from that probably aren't much greater than what they'd have been had we stayed in the USA. Parts of both cultures are virulently anti-Jewish and we've never "hidden out" in a Jewish community. On both sides of the border, we've always encouraged our children to know what non-Jewish customs are about and to be proud of our own.'

(Anonymous, Mexico)

'At one time I attended [Christian] "religious release" classes after school (at the insistence of my third grade teacher and with the approval of my father) and on Sundays attended services at the local Buddhist Temple. In the sixth grade, I declined from attending and my classmates (small K–8 [5–14 years] rural school) were a bit shocked when I replied to their inquiry that I *was* Buddhist but that I had attended in the past because my parents felt all religions were "good".'

(Fran Schwamm, Japan)

Children growing up with parents from two very different cultures may have difficulty learning much about the culture they do not live in. It is easier with two parents from the same culture who can together make a home life where their original culture has a strong position. The distances involved or political considerations may make frequent trips to the home country of the parent(s) out of the question. The children may not be able to learn enough about the second culture until they are themselves able to visit that country. In fact it may sometimes turn out that while the parents have created an oasis for their native culture at home, the children are entirely tuned into the majority culture. This may be a source of conflict in the children's teenage years, if the parents do not permit the children the same freedoms as their friends are allowed.

'I went through several phases of cultural adjustment since I'm moving back and forth between USA and Japan quite frequently since 17. While I lived in the States from 17 to 21, I tried to become "American". I never felt completely comfortable because many of the American characteristics I was trying to incorporate contradicted with what I already had, but at that time, especially when I was attending high school in the countryside, I felt it was the only way to be accepted by peers. I had another difficult time adjusting to new life when I returned to Japan, although I'm not still sure if I was struggling with Japanese culture or with a new school.'

(Aya Matsuda, Indiana)

'Definitely it has been an advantage to be bilingual, especially since the Chinese language reveals/represents Chinese culture. I identify as multicultural, having a deep appreciation of Chinese values, rituals even though I grew up in Hollywood, California, in a predominantly Euro–American area. As a child in school, there were awkward experiences of not fitting, not eating American foods, and not being a Christian/familiar with Bible readings, and not fitting the norm.'

(Donna May Wong, Oregon)

'We have had some discussions of "our home" being American vs. some of the Japanese standards he wants like his classmates. It has never been a "battle" and he seems to accept it fairly well, as is.'

(Fran Schwamm, Japan)

'We tended to follow liberal US customs. However, many Mexicans are doing the same, simply because traditional (Hispanic) Mexican child-rearing is patriarchal, matricentric and pretty brutal.'

(Harold Ormsby L., Mexico)

'We took our oldest daughter out of school and homeschooled her when she was 10. She is what I consider a "normal" child – a tomboy who loves to wrestle and climb trees, and doesn't give a hoot for what she's wearing. Well, the girls in her class told her she needed a bra, deodorant, and shaved legs – at age *10*! Also, she wasn't wearing the right kind of "cool" clothes, didn't watch TV, didn't participate in the "Pledge of Allegiance", etc. We are living near a small farming community here where everybody has a gun rack in their pickup trucks. We are currently trying to move to a nearby university town, and I hope we'll have less problems there, being "different". I know a German couple in that town, however, whose daughters are also 12 and 10 and refuse to speak German at all because none of their friends are bilingual and they don't want to be "freaks". Oh boy. I wish we could find a way to move back to Europe.'

(Gabriele Kahn, Oregon)

'My parents were quite strict and conservative and I had always believed that this was "the Japanese way"; however, since living in Japan for approximately 15 of the last 20 years, I find the Japanese are quite tolerant and indulgent with their children's behaviours.'

(Fran Schwamm, Japan)

Children's culture

There is a great deal involved in learning to behave like a native of a country. If bicultural children are to be able to feel like and pass as natives of more than one country when they are adults, then they must experience childhood in both cultures. Having a common background and shared experiences is what being a native of a particular culture is all about. Ideally, this means that the bicultural child should experience at least some of the key parts of childhood in both cultures.

Visiting a school in the second country is an enriching experience if it can be arranged, preferably at several different stages. Might it be possible for the children to go to school with a cousin or a friend's child for a day or two every other year? Such an experience gives children a window on their contemporaries' lives in the second country. They see how the children behave, how the teacher treats them, what they learn and how, and so can compare everything with how things are in their own school. The children's language will also get a boost as they learn words for things which they would never have learned at home: *blackboard*, *marker*, *break*, etc.

It is advantageous for a child to experience children's television programmes intended for children of their own age in the second culture. Apart from the language training such programmes give, they also let the child become familiar with the characters and the programmes which their contemporaries will remember fondly when they grow up. It may be possible for programmes to be viewed from another country via satellite or cable television or from video tapes recorded or bought in the second country. Shared experiences are a major part of belonging to any group. Children's literature is equally important. Reading books from both their cultures will help bicultural children to understand the culture better as well as in itself providing an experience the child will have in common with other children in each country.

Parents who are bringing up their children far away from others who share their cultural background may or may not find it natural to sing for their children so that they learn the songs and rhymes of childhood which are part of the culture of the minority language. There are many children's games, songs and even bad jokes which are passed down from older children to younger through the generations in each country. Even if children cannot attend a school in the second country or meet many children from the country, it might be possible to buy a book in which the games are described and teach them to the children.

Traditions

Whether or not to keep the traditions of the second country is a difficult question in many mixed families. Sometimes it may be possible to gather a few compatriots together to celebrate in the traditional manner. Some may settle for sharing the occasion with majority language speakers or just celebrating within the family. It is easy just to let the holiday slip by without being observed. If the majority culture also celebrates the holiday it may be easier to introduce at least some features of the minority culture. From the children's point of view, it is a shame not to share the second culture's traditions with them, even while living in another country.

Special times of year, such as Christmas, New Year, birthdays and the like often cause all attention to focus on the traditions and customs of the surrounding majority culture. In a family where the parents have different backgrounds and traditions, many questions are raised. Should Christmas be celebrated? If so, and it is part of the tradition in both countries, should it be celebrated according to the majority tradition or the minority tradition? Many families, particularly if they have young children, choose to celebrate according to both traditions, for example one country may celebrate on Christmas Eve (for example, Sweden) and the other on Christmas Day (for example, Ireland), making a two-day feast a reasonable alternative. We celebrate in the Swedish way on Christmas Eve with the Swedish cousins and their families, with cooked ham and meatballs and pickled herring and rice pudding and then invite them to celebrate with us according to Irish traditions with a turkey or goose and plum pudding on Christmas Day. Some families spend alternate years with each set of grandparents: this usually means that Christmas is celebrated in one or other way each time, but it may be possible to compromise here as so often in an intercultural relationship and take the best of both traditions in a single celebration.

Birthdays can be celebrated in different ways in different countries. Certain birthdays are considered more important than others in some places, such as 18, 21, 40 and 50. In some countries it is considered normal to throw a huge party for everyone you know on certain birthdays (e.g. your 50th birthday in Sweden), while other countries' traditions let such celebrations be kept within the family. In some countries, every day of the year is associated with one or more names. People then celebrate their name days or saint's days on the day which is associated with one of their names. Pity the poor immigrant whose foreign name is not even on the calendar! Mohammed is one of the most common names in Sweden, but it does not have a name day.

In many families it is left up to the women to keep track of birthdays and the like. For women living outside their own culture, the matter of whether or not to give presents or congratulations or send a card on a birthday or name day can be a problem. An immigrant's uncertainty as to the appropriate way to behave can look like indifference or even standoffishness.

Consider which holidays and customs from the minority language culture you feel are important for your family to celebrate. What do you want to pass on to your children? Some of these holidays may not be celebrated by the majority culture, or not in exactly the same way. It is difficult to celebrate when nobody else is celebrating. Also, you may not have the props for a traditional celebration. Whether Dutch families outside the Netherlands celebrate Sinterklaas in December, or Spanish families outside Spain celebrate the Coming of the Kings in January may depend on how much support parents get from their partner and their children to make the celebration possible. If there is a local immigrant community which shares the same culture then things get easier. We have been to a British–New Zealander Guy Fawkes Party in the depths of the Swedish countryside one year. The local American children near us in Sweden were 'trick or treating' at each other's houses at Hallowe'en long before their Swedish counterparts caught on and started doing the same. Now the Swedish shops are full of American Hallowe'en paraphernalia from mid-October, which makes it nigh on impossible to motivate children to celebrate an Irish Hallowe'en. We have, however, hosted one such memorable event, bonfire, bobbing for apples and all.

'In an effort to teach my children the cultural aspects of their American Heritage I have been very conscious of celebrating all American Holidays (Thanksgiving, Hallowe'en, St Patrick's Day, Valentine's Day, 4th of July and Christmas of course, with all its typical cultural characteristics).'

(Margo Arango, Colombia)

'We celebrate Christmas the Czech way rather than the American way, which my husband and I felt was too commercialised.' (The austere Communist Christmases in Czechoslovakia had this influence on me.) Even though my son is now 24 and my daughter 18, they still look forward to their Christmas stockings from St Nicholas and getting their gifts from Baby Jesus. We had to devise a sort of family mythology to explain the existence of Santa Claus – he had to take care of American kids, he was really Baby Jesus's helper, etc. But there was also a blending of American and Czech customs, as we adjusted to life in this country.'

(Althea Pribyl, Oregon)

'Since all of our family and extended families spend holidays together, everyone is exposed to Chinese culture – food, art, language, clothing. On the whole, all of us see multilingualism as an asset and something to achieve to enhance relationships and communication within our diverse society.'

(Donna May Wong, Oregon)

Hospitality

The way guests are treated and prepared for is another potential source of conflict in the intercultural family. On hearing that they are to have guests, the couple may react totally differently: one may be concerned with finding time to clean the house from top to bottom lest the visitors think it dirty while the other may immediately start planning menus; one may want to get the kitchen painted before the visitors come, while the other may wish to get a bigger, more expensive-looking TV-set; one may be worried about not having matching towels while the other is more concerned with how much wine the visitors are likely to drink. While some of these differences reflect individual interests, there are cultural patterns at work too, regulating how we want others to perceive us.

Guests to a Swedish home are expected to take their shoes off and walk around in their sock-soles except at the most formal parties, where they will often bring indoor shoes to wear, particularly in winter. This tradition is of course due to the unsuitable combination of bare polished wooden or vinyl floors with rag rugs and wet or snowy footwear, but really, the climate is no wetter than in England, say, where the combination of wet or muddy outdoor shoes and soft absorbent carpeting is quite unhygienic. Failure to observe the appropriate customs can cause as much resentment in one country as in the other. Woe betide dinner guests to an English home who try to take their shoes off, or visitors in Sweden who walk in with their shoes on leaving tracks on the floor! Nothing might be said, it being known that the offender is a foreigner, but if looks could kill. . .

Away from home too, out at the pub or a restaurant, the matter of who pays for what varies in different cultures. Some never allow a woman to pay for anything, others 'go Dutch': even the expression reflects a cultural difference. Some have a culture of 'buying rounds' with strict turn-taking rules, while others have everybody counting out their own share of the bill, even at a restaurant. Failure to be aware of the appropriate behaviour can cause resentment and a breakdown in communication.

These differences are part of the adult culture and very difficult to teach explicitly. In addition, these kinds of unwritten rules are liable to change as years go by, so parents who have not lived in their native culture for many years may be quite old-fashioned in their behaviour. The best way for children and young people to prepare for a period in the 'other' country is to be aware that things will be different from what they are at home and to keep their eyes and ears open and do what others do. This advice is, of course, appropriate for any young people going abroad. The difference is that youngsters who have grown up with the language spoken in the country they are going to visit may speak the language with little or no foreign accent or lack of fluency and therefore be expected to behave like native speakers.

Food and drink

Food and drink can be a source of difficulty for the family with two cultures. In southern Europe, for example, it is considered perfectly normal for even quite young children to drink wine mixed with water. In Scandinavia such a practice would be considered scandalous and may even be illegal. In some countries, the evening meal is served very late, and children stay up late at night, while people in other countries eat much earlier and have children in bed by 7 or 8 p.m. The kinds of food served may be very characteristic of the culture. Mixed families often come up with a compromise on the question of what kind of food they eat, taking the best from each tradition. The children may well be used to the food eaten in both the country they live in and the country that one parent comes from. This is because immigrants often miss the food they are used to and see to it that they can at least sometimes eat the familiar dishes of their childhood. In doing so, they automatically pass the culinary tradition of their home country on to their children. There may be some things that you feel are important to pass on to your children. Our children, for example, have been brought up with jelly and ice-cream at birthday parties, to the amazement (and sometimes disgust) of their Swedish friends, and occasional feeds of Irish potato bread (very popular even with Swedes!).

Eating and drinking are major parts of the culture of a people, and this is certainly reflected in the daily life of the intercultural couple. If only one of them shops and cooks, there may be more of that side's culinary tradition represented, but not necessarily. Many families find that their eating habits gravitate towards a mixture of food from the majority and the minority culture, at least if it is the immigrant who does the cooking. Otherwise there will probably be a lot more majority culture food.

Many people really learn to cook only when they set up house on their own, and if that is in a country other than where they were brought up, then that will be reflected in the food they eat. For an immigrant with a partner from the majority culture much can be learned about the majority culture's food. You need to learn to shop for food in a new way: even if you might be able to find enough familiar food from your home country, it will be imported and therefore expensive. You may have to learn to eat like the people of the majority culture if your grocery bills are not to get out of control. This is not to say that you need to totally turn your back on the cooking methods and ingredients you are familiar with, but you may need to adapt recipes to locally available foodstuffs, and save authentic specialities from your childhood for special occasions.

Men and women

In all cultures, even those which profess to have totally gone beyond any kind of gender-bound thinking, the relationship between men and women is fundamental, but it works differently in different cultures. While women in some countries may feel financially and socially obliged to work full time outside the home and leave their toddlers in day-care, women in other countries are financially and socially able to and expected to stay at home with their children until they start school. The intercultural family may find that their expectations of how men or women behave are not always met.

Men and women have different areas of responsibility in different cultures, although individual differences may be considerable: potential areas of conflict may include childcare, cooking, housework, practical house-repair work, shopping for food and clothes and economic responsibility. These issues are sensitive, and difficult to discuss for many people, although they will be important to the way the children are to be raised. The family may need to be aware of cultural differences between what they see, for example, as boys' and girls' education, chores, pastimes and toys. For some fathers it may be important that they are able to pass on to their sons knowledge given them by their fathers, be it about football, how to tickle a trout, how to put up wallpaper or how to judge which trees in a forest to fell first. Mothers may have similar knowledge to pass on to their daughters, about traditional crafts, how to make traditional foodstuffs or traditional ways of dressing.

There are, however, advantages to growing up in an intercultural family. It is a way to learn about other people and to understand that there is really very little that can be taken for granted. The adults involved also come to see their own culture through new eyes, and may become more broad-minded in the process. It is not for everybody. Anybody looking for a simple life would do much better to marry the boy or girl next door! Many adults who themselves grew up with two languages report mixed experiences of being exposed to two cultures.

'I think I fit into other cultures better since I have practical, almost daily experience of moving from one to another.'

(Jasmin Harvey, USA)

'For me, being multicultural has meant that I'm not clearly "from" anywhere; not that that's a problem, necessarily. When I was a college student here in the States, I found the questions and comments of my monocultural peers unbearably predictable (cute accent, there was an exchange student from Finland in my high school, etc.). There isn't a convenient category people can plug me in, so in those early years I tended to find myself repeating my entire weird family history over and over to near strangers – or even total strangers. Now I just don't do that for them; if someone *must* know "where I'm from" I tell some convenient part of the story. I'm not obligated to help them categorise me. Lately, I've managed to blend in, so most people don't realise how strange my background is.'

(Mai Kuha, USA)

Chapter 8

Problems you may encounter

Quality of input

If children are to acquire two languages they need to hear enough of both languages spoken directly to them (i.e. sitting a child in front of a television programme in the target language will not generally be enough). But if children are regularly spoken to by non-native speakers of the language they will probably pick up features of their speech. Some parents are concerned about speaking their non-native language in front of the children (even if not speaking directly to the children) lest the children pick up non-native characteristics from the parent's speech. In the case of the minority language parent speaking the majority language, there is probably no need to worry. Most children hear so many native speakers of the majority language that they will probably not use any erroneous pronunciations, words or grammar that they pick up from their minority language parent. Even if a small child copies a parent's foreign accent in the majority language, this will generally be replaced by a local accent as the child's social circle grows.

In the case of the minority language, it might be better for children to hear even non-native speakers if this means that they also hear more native speech in the minority language. In other words, the child will hear the minority language speaking mother more often if she speaks her language both directly to the child and also when she speaks to the child's father. This more than makes up for the possibility of the child picking up the father's foreign accent in the minority language. Our experience is that children soon become aware of which parent makes mistakes in a language and will join the native-speaking parent in pointing out errors.

Losing a language

Even the parent who is a native speaker of a language may not always be an error-free language model. After years without much contact with other native speakers, particularly native speakers who do not know the majority language, you might feel that your proficiency in your first language is no longer what it was. Unusual words may have disappeared from your active vocabulary and even from your passive vocabulary. Doing crosswords or playing Scrabble with friends from your youth who stayed at home can be a real eye-opener, and may make you realise just how far behind your advanced vocabulary has fallen.

The speech of those who have lived abroad for many years is sometimes quaint and full of out-of-date expressions. Words referring to technological advances are also problematic; you may know them well enough in the language of your new country, but how do you say them in your native language? The same goes for experiences you have had in your new language, such as having a baby or learning a sport: you can say it all in the new language, but you may just not have the appropriate vocabulary in your native language. For example, are car windows toned or tinted? Do you leave your children in day-care or childcare or what?

'Of course my first language is affected! I speak a much simpler English than before. Sometimes I just cannot find that one word that eludes me. ... Part of me now views people with extensive vocabularies as pretentious and the other part of me is jealous.'

(American woman living in Sweden)

'Fortunately I use Japanese at work. This helps a lot to preserve my language skill. However, my Japanese has "frozen" since I left Japan nine years ago. If I speak to people in Japan now my Japanese may sound slightly out of date.'

(Kaori Matsuda, Australia)

Once you have become proficient in your second language, you may find that the patterns of that language pervade your thinking and the way you plan what to say next. You may say something which superficially appears to be in your native language, and which may go unnoticed if you are speaking to others who share your linguistic situation or to native speakers of the majority language, but which a monolingual speaker of your native language might totally fail to understand. In this case, you have probably made a direct translation of an idiom of the majority language without recognising it as such. You are in an even worse situation than a native speaker of the majority language, who would probably avoid trying to translate such idioms into another language. Your use of such constructions in your so-called native language will legitimise them in the eyes of your children.

There is evidence to suggest that it is not possible to become native-like in a second language without cost to your first language. Major (1990) studied American women who had lived in Brazil for many years. He found that the better their pronunciation of Portuguese, the greater the effect on their pronunciation of English. Major measured tiny differences in the way that the women pronounced <t>, <d> and <k> in English and Portuguese in both formal and casual speech. The women were in fact starting to pronounce English consonants in a way that was not quite American and not quite Portuguese, almost as though they were developing tendencies towards Portuguese accents in their English.

Any effect that a majority language has on an immigrant's native language is intrinsically undesirable. This is particularly so when immigrants are trying to pass on their native language to their children and the target is to have the child become proficient in the language as it is spoken in the parent's country of origin. However, even less than perfectly native input is infinitely better than none.

What to do about language attrition?

We posted a question to the Internet mailing list TESL-L (see Appendix D) for teachers of English as a second language (which actually has many members who are involved with teaching English as a *foreign* language, i.e. not in a country where English is spoken) asking what members of the list did to keep from losing their English while living abroad. The 25 answers we received gave many helpful tips:

- Several people recommended listening to radio broadcasts in English, and reading books and magazines.
- One had relatives send clippings from newspapers and magazines with examples of current slang and idiom.

- Another felt that his English might actually have improved while abroad since teaching and translation work focus attention on the language.

- An American in Turkey felt that the lack of contact with native speakers in combination with teaching English had produced a hyper-correct form of English (with, for example, overly clear enunciation).

- Several replies pointed out the value of British and American television shows for gleaning current usage.

- Some people suggested trying to find newcomers, who are still uninfluenced by the majority language, or speakers of English as a second language who have a language other than the majority language as their first language.

- One American who has been living in France for the past 25 years reported that he tries to think as though he was at home, for example when he answers the phone he says what he would have said if he had never left home. He also advised answering in English anybody who speaks English to you, even if their English is poor, making no allowance for their difficulties: 'We're not in class now!' he wrote.

- Another English speaker who has lived in France for over 20 years reported being less than thrilled when he was complimented in Canada on how well he spoke English. He recommended listening to the radio and reading as well as keeping a vocabulary book to learn neologisms and forgotten metaphors.

- Reading English books aloud to your children and doing crosswords were other recommendations, as well as reading recent novels.

- Many replies pointed out that just being aware of the problem was half the battle.

> 'I am very grateful to my children for allowing me to continue with my native language on a daily basis. I am sure it would have severely suffered otherwise. I can only take what the English only (or mainly) environment does to my academic German as an indication of what would happen to my "private" German if it wasn't for them.'
>
> (Susanne Döpke, Australia – author of
> One Parent, One Language: An Interactional Approach, 1992)

'My German has considerably deteriorated through the continuous use of English. This became apparent when in 1983 my father read something I had written in German and published. He corrected all the syntax and punctuation, as well as some aspects of vocabulary. The mistakes were recognisable to me and a clear indication of how much I had lost the accuracy of my German.'

(German man living in England)

Semilingualism

The term *semilingual* is sometimes used to refer to individuals, often second generation immigrants, who are said to lack native-speaker competence in either of their languages. Skutnabb-Kangas (1981) and Hansegård (1975) are associated with the term 'semilingualism'. This is the worst case scenario that haunts many parents who are bringing up their children with two languages. Romaine (1995: 261–265) explains how the notion developed in connection with the study of the language skills of ethnic minorities. Semilingualism implies a comparison with some kind of idealised full competence in a language. Romaine explains this view in terms of what she calls 'the container view of competence' (1995: 264). An ideal adult monolingual speaker has a 'full container', while an ideal adult bilingual has two full containers; a semilingual adult has two less than full containers. She relates this to Lambert's (1975) notion of the balanced bilingual, i.e. one who has equal though not necessarily full knowledge of two languages. The notion of semilingualism has been dismissed by researchers as being due to a mistaken view of cognitive development, and partly due to the techniques used to test the linguistic development of children with two languages. The discussion has concerned speakers in bilingual communities rather than the kind of individual bilingual situation we describe in this book.

The notion of semilingualism has generally been rejected. It is, nonetheless, very common for children who grow up with two languages to have difficulty in the minority language (for example, foreign accent, limited vocabulary, non-native grammar, etc.). This is usually due to their limited exposure to the minority language, and will generally improve if they are in a situation with more input in that language. Some of these children might have subtle problems with the majority language, for example, with gaps in their vocabulary. This cannot, however, be attributed solely to the child's bilingual situation. Most children find ways to compensate for not hearing the majority language in all kinds of situations, for example, through their majority language schoolwork and social contacts or in their own reading. But children who avoid reading and who do not do well in school for reasons unconnected to their linguistic situation may be left with a less than monolingual-like command of the majority language. Of course, it is impossible to know how an individual's command of the majority language would have been if he had never been exposed to a minority language.

Most parents, teachers and linguists would agree that it is absolutely essential for the children who grow up with two languages to have at least one language which they know very well. It is often assumed that the majority language must necessarily be the dominant language. This is certainly the usual way, and probably most advantageous to the child who is being schooled through the medium of the majority language. If the child is being educated in the minority language at home or at an international school, then that language may be dominant. It is generally expected that the dominant language at least will be mastered without any foreign accent and in every other way be equivalent to a monolingual's native language.

For some second generation immigrant youngsters in the inner cities things do not work out this way: they end up sounding non-native in both their languages. Research in Sweden (Kotsinas 1994) indicates that a new variety of Swedish may, in fact, be emerging, spoken by young people who live in areas of Swedish cities where native Swedish speakers are a tiny minority, and many languages are spoken. Swedish becomes a lingua franca, but, with few native speakers around to model, the language develops in new directions, borrowing words from many different immigrant languages. This is not to say that these speakers cannot or do not also learn standard Swedish.

For a small number of children, even those brought up with two languages in circumstances which would appear to favour the majority language, the second or minority language may influence the dominant or majority language. Children with two languages have quite simply more to learn. If these children are to have a satisfactory command of at least one and preferably both of their languages, both the children and the parents, and ideally also the children's teachers, will have to work at it. Those well-meaning strangers who comment on how great it is that the children get a second language for free do not know what they are saying.

Of course, all children do not have problems. Very many parents and teachers feel that their children are indistinguishable from monolingual children in their dominant (majority) language.

Changed circumstances

For one reason or another, things do not always go according to plan. No matter how well a couple thought through how they wanted to handle their child's linguistic development with two languages, things do not always turn out as they expected. People move away, get divorced, or die, thwarting the bilingual family's arrangements. In some cases external events may play havoc with the lives of individuals. Perhaps employment or domestic matters force a family to move to another country or to move back to a country where one or both of the parents came from. This means that they may need to modify their plans and targets for their children's language acquisition. A family moving back to the country where both parents originate from must decide whether they will try to maintain their children's (and indeed their own) level of competence in the majority language of the country they are leaving. If they are going on to another overseas position where there will be a new language and culture to learn, most will probably put their language skills to work to help them to learn the new language, rather than try to maintain a language that they no longer need in their daily life.

A family who is not likely to live abroad again may try to keep up the children's language. One way to do this is by employing an au-pair from that country. A couple we knew, both from Northern Ireland, had lived many years in Sweden and finally left to live in England with their three children (all born in Sweden). They were unsure whether they would want to return to Sweden or not, and wanted to keep their options open. They came up with the ingenious scheme of bringing one of the helpers at their children's Swedish pre-school back with them to England as an au-pair.

Divorce

There is no shortage of reasons why a mixed language, intercultural couple might come into conflict with each other. The odds are really stacked against them. In addition to their cultural differences, linguistic confusion may compound the partners' lack of common ground with misunderstandings and misinterpretations of what the other says and an inability to express themselves so the other can read both the message and what is written between the lines. However, both partners go into the relationship with their eyes open, even if love is blind. They are likely to be aware of the problems; the only issue is whether they can find ways to live with them or if they allow the difficulties of an intercultural relationship to overshadow the advantages.

The breakdown of any relationship can be a tragedy for those involved. In the intercultural relationship, the stakes may be higher. If one partner has left his or her home country to move to the other's country, what is that partner to do if the relationship collapses? Depending on the terms of the particular country's immigration legislation, the foreign partner may or may not be allowed to stay in the new country. (In Sweden, for example, a permanent residence permit is usually granted to love-immigrants after three years – before that they must leave if the relationship ends.) If it is possible to stay in the country, the immigrant is faced with a number of decisions. The individual circumstances of the immigrant's work and the possibility of getting work in the home country will presumably influence the decision.

The real problems start when there are children involved. They may not have any interest in uprooting and moving to their mother's or father's country of origin and away from any possibility of reasonable access to the other parent. An immigrant parent who decides to stay in the other parent's country will need to make a new life alone or with the children. This can be difficult if the native partner has been the one to deal with the authorities and the family's administration; however, many native divorcees are in a similar position.

For some, it may not be possible to return to their country of origin. This might be because they have relinquished their original nationality to adopt that of their new country, so that they no longer have any right of residence in their country of origin. Others may feel that they have been away from their original country for so long that it no longer feels like home. Some may come from cultures where the stigma of being divorced is so great that it makes a life in exile appear to be a more attractive option. For those who left their home country against the wishes of their parents, going back after the relationship's breakdown might feel like the ultimate failure and loss of face.

Other problems arise for the children of a mixed language couple who get divorced. If the minority language speaking parent no longer lives with the children, it may be difficult for them to get enough input in the minority language. This is especially true if the minority language speaking parent moves back to his or her country of origin. Even making trips to the minority parent's new home may not be enough to let the children continue their bilingual development. However, if the trips are frequent and long enough, these children may be better able to acquire both languages and cultures than they would have been if their parents had not divorced. They can see both languages in the context of their associated cultures; both parents are fully linguistically and culturally competent. The children see both cultures and languages at their best.

> 'My two older children still speak Dutch with their father whom they see for about six weeks each year, and we read Dutch books together, and sometimes I speak Dutch with them. They haven't lost their fluency so far.'
>
> (Gabriele Kahn, Oregon)
>
> 'I had to fight hard to get the children for as many as 12 days a month (every Tuesday night, and from Thursday night to Sunday night, twice a month). One of my principal motivations was to establish a regular English language and cultural environment for them.'
>
> (Sean Golden, Barcelona)

If it is the majority language speaking parent who moves away from the children, the position is different. The minority language speaking parent may wish to return to the country of origin taking the children along. The other parent may oppose such a move on the grounds that his or her relationship with the children would be made very difficult. The children might forget the language if they move to a country where they have no contact with speakers of that language. Otherwise, if the minority language speaking parent remains in the country the family lived in before the divorce, he or she will be left with a monolingual minority language home. In some cases, this might strengthen the children's minority language skills, but it is unlikely to be generally beneficial to the children, given the reduced amount of time that single parents are generally able to spend with their children.

In some cases it has happened that minority language parents have taken the children away to their home country against the will of the other parent, even if they did not have custody of the children. Sometimes these cases are brought to trial as kidnapping, and parents can be denied any access to their children for many years. These extreme breakdowns in the relationship between parents are more likely to occur when there are significant cultural and religious differences.

Death of a parent

The death of a parent while a child is growing up is always tragic, especially for young children. In addition to all the other effects it will have, a parent's death in a mixed language family may result in severe problems with the children's linguistic development, especially in the case of the loss of the minority language speaking parent. This language may suddenly disappear from the children's lives. In such a case, visits to grandparents and cousins in the deceased parent's home country are valuable and may be a way forward for the children. Much depends on how old they are when they lose their parent.

In the event of the majority parent's remarriage, unexpected challenges may arise especially if the new spouse is a fellow native of the country of residence. Children who are used to a certain kind of upbringing and cooking may not have realised how much their way of life was influenced by their deceased parent's foreign culture. They may be surprised to be exposed to an undiluted dose of the majority culture at home, and miss their other parent's language and ways almost as much as they miss the parent. Most mixed language families live a life which has features of both traditions. The children may not be able to maintain their minority language skills in such a situation, unless their other parent is very motivated to help them.

Adjusting to setbacks

Some children may simply be frustrated by the whole idea of two languages, like the little boy in the following comment:

> 'I was raised speaking French and English in Brooklyn, NY. My parents spoke French at home, and we learned English in school and with our peers. My brother tried to raise his children bilingually, but his son, at the age of 4, rejected the whole idea by yelling once: "The words, they're stuck in my throat, they won't come out".'
>
> (Helene Ossipov, Arizona)

Children with one, two or more languages go through any number of phases in their use of their languages as in other aspects of their development. A major problem at the age of 3 may have completely disappeared by 3½, replaced by another new problem: children's developmental phases usually do not last for ever. The parents in the above example gave up their attempt to let the child acquire French, one of his father's two languages. They may or may not have made a wise choice: only the parents are really in a position to decide what is best for their child. There are, however, a number of ways to help children get over a temporary problem.

The most important way to help your children is to ensure that they get as much input as possible in both languages. Another way to help is to be consistent in who speaks which language, especially at the beginning. A child will find it easier to sort out the two languages if there is some logic behind the choice of which language is used. Later on, many parents feel that they do not have to be quite as consistent and may, for example, speak the majority language to the child when guests are present.

Many parents find that their children sooner or later begin to answer them in the majority language, even when addressed in the minority language. This is not a reason to give up, just a minor and temporary setback. There are several methods that parents have used successfully to thwart this majority language intrusion. Probably the most effective way is to take the children to a country where they will hear only the minority language for a week or two, preferably without taking a majority language speaking parent along! This is often enough to turn things around and restore the child–parent dialogue in the minority language. Other methods which we have found useful, but which may or may not help, are the following:

- Remind the child to speak the minority language. Often children are just so eager to say what they have on their minds that they are unwilling to take the time or make the effort to use the minority language, which is probably their weaker language. A gentle prompt might be enough to encourage them back to the minority language.
- Repeat back what the child said but using the minority language, in much the same way as a parent corrects and expands the speech of a much younger child. For example, if the child says in Swedish 'Får jag åka och bada med Niklas?' (Can I go swimming with Niklas?) to his mother with whom he is 'supposed' to speak English, the mother might say: 'Do you want to go swimming with Niklas?'

- An alternative is to refuse to answer the child until he or she uses the appropriate language. This will not be a suitable tactic for some children, and should be used in a spirit of fun rather than force.
- A milder variant is to say in the appropriate language something like 'Sorry, what was that you said?' This should not be taken too far. Some children will become thoroughly frustrated if they are not allowed to express themselves in the language of their choice. It might work to try to wear the child's resistance down by, as often as seems reasonable, reacting when they use the 'wrong' language, but not going on at them about it, and not refusing to listen to what they are trying to say. Children need to feel that they can talk to their parents. You know your child, do what you think will work!

'Kids will become as proficient as they need to be, and no more, in both languages. Language proficiency can be increased at any point in life.'

(Harold Ormsby L., Mexico)

'My only advice to others is to do what feels natural. Don't follow anyone else's advice.'

(Nancy Holm, Sweden)

'Remember that some kids may well not want to be bilingual. It is, after all, a personal decision. They may be happy enough to know another language (anyway, once a language is in your head, you can't get it out) but they may not want to use it. In general, these kids will prefer the language of the society around them. In some cases, this may be "a phase"; in others, it may be a decision for life. In either case, I think parents should respect the kid's decision.'

(Harold Ormsby L., Mexico)

Redefining targets

Eventually, many parents find that they are obliged to lower the level of ambition they had at the beginning concerning their child's bilingual development. If they had envisaged a balanced bilingual with monolingual-like knowledge of two languages and cultures, they may find that their child by the age of 10 is a pretty well monolingual-like speaker of the majority language with some level of knowledge of the minority language. Even if the child is reluctant to speak the minority language, an extensive passive knowledge can be maintained if the parent perseveres with speaking the minority language to the child as often as possible. This passive knowledge can be built upon at a later stage. If the child is at all willing to use the minority language, the parents can feel very pleased with themselves.

Even speech full of interference from the majority language is an invaluable asset to the child, allowing them access to the minority language speaking side of the family, as well as the associated culture. Such a child has the potential to become very competent in their second language given an opportunity to use it in a setting where it is the majority language. The key to success is not to give up, even in the face of adversity, and to adapt to changes in the way most beneficial to the child.

Children with special needs

Other setbacks to the parents' plans may arise if they find that one or more of their children has a specific difficulty with languages. Children are individuals, and some learn language more easily than others. Some children may have special needs, such as hearing deficiencies or developmental disorders. Parents of these children may need to re-evaluate their position, and perhaps modify the targets they have more or less consciously set up for their children's linguistic and general development.

On an intuitive level you might feel that children born from the genetic melting pot of a mixed marriage should be extraordinarily healthy individuals. Unfortunately there is no guarantee of this: disabled children are born in families with two languages just as in families with a single language. There are many disabilities that can affect children's ability to deal with language, for example deafness, Down's Syndrome, dyslexia, attention deficit hyperactivity disorder (ADHD), autism and other learning disabilities.

Deaf children are usually taught sign language as their first language, and may subsequently learn something of the mainstream majority spoken language (at least in its written form). They are thus brought up bilingually in sign language and the spoken language. In a family where more than one language is spoken, arrangements may have to be made to allow the deaf child to concentrate on a single spoken language. Two languages to be acquired in addition to sign language is probably an unrealistic target without the benefit of hearing. The family needs to decide which of the spoken languages the child will use more. If the family does not intend to move, the majority language is likely to be more useful to the child in daily dealings with the health services and aides. If the family plans to move to another country in the future, for example back to the parents' homeland, they might need to rethink, or to bring the move forward in time, to save the deaf child from a language switch. Similar problems are faced by parents of children with other disabilities.

Examples

An English-speaking couple were living in Sweden when their first child was born with Down's Syndrome. Both parents spoke English to the child in the beginning, and she learned some Swedish at her day-care and in the course of all the various therapy sessions she attended. Eventually the family intended returning to England, but they returned earlier than planned to spare their daughter the additional complication of bilingualism. These children have enough to cope with in one language. It seems unnecessary to burden them with two. But there are families and children for whom there is no alternative but to battle on with two languages.

A child in a mixed language (English–Swedish) family has autism. His language delay was considerable in both languages. At the age of 2 he used only a few words (mixed Swedish and English). When he was 3 his English was clearly dominant; much of his language was taken from videos. In fact, he used only English in his communication outside the family, for example to his pre-school teachers. Now, at 6 his Swedish has taken over (and has actually caught up so that his language is very nearly normal for his age). He understands English well, but will generally answer in Swedish. He gets away with this without pressure to speak English, but he is fully aware that he will need to speak English when he goes to visit his grandparents. The family has persevered with the one person–one language method with him as with their other children, and are now satisfied that that was the best solution for him and for the entire family.

Seeing the signs

Some children are late talkers. This is true of children growing up with one, two or more languages. It may be the case for some children that their language delay is caused by having two languages. The children are expected to learn twice as much, but given the same total amount of stimulation and help from their parents. Language delay usually means that the child is trying to make rules for the way the languages work. There is no evidence that this kind of delay has any long-term effects on the child's speech.

It is, nonetheless, important to be just as observant about a lack of speech or other problem with language development in a child exposed to two languages as in any other child, and have the child's hearing and development checked if you are worried. Do not let yourself be reassured by other parents who tell you about children they have known (with or without two languages) who did not speak until they were much older than your child and who went on to speak beautifully. If *you* are concerned about your child's language development, do have the child checked up. If there is no need to be concerned, it will put your mind at rest, but some late-talking children do have hearing or other developmental problems. The earlier these conditions are discovered the better.

Chapter 9

The way ahead

Motivation

The single most important factor in raising children with two languages (as, indeed, in any other language learning situation) is motivation. Without a good reason, the effort required to learn a language is simply not worth making. Children, at least after a certain age, need to be motivated to accept being spoken to in the minority language and to make the attempt to answer their parent in this language. Parents need to be motivated, at first to accommodate their children into the couple's language system in such a way that they will be systematically exposed to both languages, and later to ensure that they get sufficient direct interaction in each language. Both the parents and the children will find that their levels of motivation will fluctuate. One or other parent may spend less time with the children than the other; the children may be away from home most of the time. The family language system must be flexible enough to adapt to the family's changing circumstances. If the system breaks down for any reason, for example, a change in the family's country or even city of residence, a divorce or bereavement, a new system must be devised to replace it.

Promote children's self-image as speakers of the minority language

A belief in oneself is a powerful tool. Children who are encouraged in their use of the minority language and praised for their proficiency will quickly come to see themselves as speakers of that language. They may, of course, be disappointed when they realise that they are not actually indistinguishable from monolingual peers, but they are much more likely to want to communicate in the minority language if they believe that they do it well. The converse is, naturally, also true. Children who are corrected overly often or teased for making mistakes in the minority language will be reluctant to speak it and will be unsure of their ability to communicate using the language. Such children may well turn their backs entirely on the second language.

Work systematically with your children

If your children are not getting any help with their minority language in the community or their school, you may want to try to support them in an academic way at home. For pre-school children you may be able to find early learning books produced to let monolingual parents and children practise concepts such as reading, writing, counting and colours in the minority language.

With children from the age of 7 or 8 you may want to work through the kinds of material that children use in their language work in a country where the minority language is spoken. If you can find a way to motivate your children to study their weaker language, this kind of work can be valuable. Perhaps you can contact teachers in your home country and ask what books they recommend. You may need to use books meant for slightly younger children. Most children with two languages are not quite up to the level of their monolingual peers in the minority language. If you can get hold of books intended for home-schooling, these might be suitable. You may like to set up a regular time for the child to work with you in the minority language, maybe for a couple of hours on Saturday or Sunday mornings, and then again for a couple of hours on the evening they have least homework. If you have more than one schoolchild, let them study the minority language together. They might not make a class, but they can work together on some things. Avoid competition between them if that is a problem.

It can be difficult to make this kind of extra study at home work without some external motivation or target. We have personally had only sporadic success on this front, generally on the children's own initiative after they have been in Ireland or in some other situation where they have seen the benefit of proficiency in English. Their enthusiasm has soon waned when they realise how much they have to learn. Other parents we know have been better able to regularly home-school their children in the minority language. How important you feel this is will depend on your family situation and your children's inclinations and abilities.

Teenagers

As children grow older they may be less likely to want to speak the minority language. Pleasing a parent is, for many young people, no longer sufficient motivation for making an extra effort or being different. If the minority language is a school language, both young people who have grown up with the language and their schoolmates may see the value of being proficient, although some may find that being better than the rest of the class is an embarrassment in itself. One of the major advantages we have found with bilingual and English-medium education is that all the children in the class are in the same boat – speaking English is not 'different' in such an environment.

Using the minority language

Some parents find that while they were able to give their children the kind of linguistic input they needed to learn to speak the minority language when they were young, there comes a point where they are not able to develop their language further. The level of language proficiency expected of a young adult is simply more than it is possible to achieve in a setting where the language is represented by a single parent or a handful of speakers. If young people are to develop their language further it will have to be through contacts with other speakers of the language. Some of these contacts can be one way, for example, through the written word in newspapers, magazines and books or through radio and television programmes in the minority language. Newspapers and magazines can be subscribed to or are available through the Internet. Books in many languages can be bought (for example, via the Internet) or borrowed from libraries. TV and radio in the minority language may be available via satellite or cable or the Internet.

If a young person who has actively used the minority language suddenly stops and chooses to answer the minority language speaking parent in the majority language, it is worth attempting to reverse this decision. There are several approaches which might work:

- What kind of career does the young person envisage? There may be some way to associate the desired career with the minority language. Young people who dream of being, for example, a journalist have two markets for their work if they have sufficient facility in two languages. Perhaps you could help such youngsters to access magazines and papers in the minority language (possibly through the Internet) to show that there are speakers of the minority language who share their interests. If, for example, a career in banking is the goal, knowledge of two languages and cultures is an asset. A prospective teacher can either teach in a country where the minority language is spoken or be a resource for the pupils with two languages in the majority language country. A young person who plans to work in tourism or other service jobs will find the minority language useful sooner or later.

- What are your teenagers' interests? Is it possible to put them in touch with peers in a country where the minority language is spoken who share the same interests?
- The ultimate motivation for using a language is to need it to communicate. Would it be possible to send your teenager to the country where the minority language is spoken? This could be to go to school or college there for a period, to work, for example, for a summer job, or just to visit relations or friends there.
- In the case of English, we have motivated a 10-year-old to read English books (with the help of a taped reading) by pointing out that a native-like command of the language is within his grasp. We also mentioned that being a native speaker of English (in combination with a good general education) is enough to live on in many parts of the world.
- Consider bribery or reward schemes, or anything you can think of.

Even if a child or teenager answers in the majority language, there is still a tremendous amount to be won by persevering with the minority language, at least at home. Regularly being addressed in the minority language will often be enough to ensure that the young person has a passive command of the language. This can relatively easily be turned into an active command when required, for example when there is a communicative need for it, such as on a visit to a country where the minority language is spoken. If the language is not a part of the family's daily life, the children's knowledge of it will be difficult to maintain.

It may not always be possible to carry on using the minority language, especially if it has been actively rejected by the children. In some cases parents may find that the pressure from the majority language is too great and go over entirely to using the majority language in the family. In families where the minority language is a school language the loss might not feel too great – the young people will at least bé able to keep up the language through school. In other cases the loss might be total and the youngsters might be cutting themselves off from a part of their background which they will come to miss.

Identity

The language that people choose to use can be an expression of where they stand. Teenagers who have grown up with a minority language can easily mark their independence from their parents and their rejection of parental values by choosing not to speak the minority language. There is a good deal said about the difficulties faced by young people who grow up with two cultures. In some cases they may be left feeling like outsiders in both the majority and the minority cultures. The first aim is generally to ensure that they feel like full members of the majority culture in which they live. A secondary aim is to enable them to feel at home in the country where one or both their parents are from. If there is a subculture made up of youngsters from similar immigrant backgrounds, that may be where these young people feel most at home.

Children of mixed parentage are often described as being half this and half that. This is a very negative way of looking at their dual linguistic and cultural affiliation. We have taught our children to think of themselves as *both* Swedish and Irish. Their Irishness must not be allowed to detract from their Swedishness (or vice versa). One problem with this is that they are sometimes called upon to represent Ireland – at the international school, for example, they are referred to as the Irish children. This is quite a burden to bear considering the limited amount of time they have spent there.

Teenagers are often concerned with finding their place in life. Being brought up in two cultures might give them a bit more to think about. The image of the young person with full linguistic and cultural competence in two languages with their associated cultures is not usually attainable in reality. However, if the teenager has active or passive skills in the minority language, perhaps steps can be taken to fill in the cultural gaps left in the minority culture by a childhood in another country. Many teenagers, even without a bilingual upbringing, spend a term or a year in a school or college abroad. This could be an excellent way for young people from a mixed or immigrant family to become more familiar with the culture associated with their second language and to bring their language skills up to scratch.

Some teenagers may feel that they need to choose between their two cultural allegiances. They need to know where they 'belong'. They might orient themselves aggressively towards the majority language/culture in the country where they live, or they might feel a strong affiliation with the minority language and culture, and go on to study that language more and maybe live in the country. Others can happily accept that they have two parallel backgrounds, cultures and languages. The problem then is deciding which side to support in international sports competitions!

Grown-up children

Improving language proficiency

Depending on the circumstances of their childhood, people who grew up with two languages will have varying levels of proficiency in their two languages. It is possible for them as adults to improve their language skills. People who grew up with a passive knowledge of a minority language may find that a visit to the country where the language is spoken can push them to be active speakers. They may find that they know much more of the language than they thought.

A person with very little knowledge of the minority language may want to learn the language as an adult. In some cases such adult learners might find that they can learn to speak the minority language easily and with good pronunciation.

Those who were active speakers of both languages throughout childhood and adolescence may be able to use their languages regularly at work or in their spare time. It is easy to let one of the languages fall into disuse if opportunities to use it are not sought out.

Grandchildren

When those who grew up with two languages become parents themselves they may or may not choose to pass on both their languages. This decision will depend partly on the young family's linguistic situation. Are both parents proficient in both languages? Where do they live? Does the parent who grew up with two languages feel confident of his or her ability to be a good language model?

There may be pressure from the minority language speaking grand-parent (or grandparents) to pass on the second language. A grandmother who has devoted years to helping her son or daughter to become a competent speaker of her native language may be disappointed if she cannot communicate with her grandchildren in the same language. In some situations the answer may be to involve the minority language speaking grandparent in the linguistic upbringing of the child. If they meet often enough (at least several times a week from the child's first year) the grandmother may be able to establish her native language with the child.

If the other parent does not speak or even understand the minority language, it might be difficult to arrange this kind of system. In such circumstances the aim of giving a grandchild a second language from childhood is probably not worth the friction it might cause in the young family.

Advice from other parents

We asked other parents raising children with two languages in many countries what advice they would give to those starting out. Their answers are often contradictory and reflect each individual family's situation and experience. No one solution will work for everyone. Take what you can use from the advice offered!

'It's a little like feeding a child; offer a rich assortment of experiences, books, tapes, friends, acquaintances, travel, stay with relatives, anything. But do not force feed.'

(Thomas Beyer, USA)

'
- Parents should use their native language(s) to the child, rather than deliberately trying to teach the child a particular language. They should realise that the child will pick up the community language without being taught it.
- Parents in such situations should demand bilingual education as a right. If the minority language is too much of a minority for this to be feasible it will need special effort to keep it up. If it is only used in the home, the child will never develop fully fledged skills including literacy in the language.
- Keep a diary of the child's language, noting striking usages such as mixing and transfer. It will be a source of great amusement later, and be invaluable for diagnosis if problems should develop.

It is probably significant that our son's best friend at school is a "bilingual" Eurasian girl. Without such company he could easily feel like an outsider among monolingual Cantonese children.'

(Steve Matthews, Hong Kong)

'Be strict about establishing the non-community language as the language of the home. Do not switch languages. If one parent is not proficient in the foreign language it is best for that parent to stick to his/her native language. Provide opportunities for the child to hear the non-community language, by, for example, getting a weekly play-group together with other mothers/fathers and children who speak the language you are trying to teach your child. Children's TV programmes in the language can be good; although TV is a passive medium, the kids can pick new vocabulary up. Read, read, read, every night as a bedtime routine. Being in a foreign culture, exposure to that culture is automatic. This is not a problem. It is important not to lead the children into thinking that one culture is superior to another in your effort to teach your language and culture. A balance must be kept in order for that child to be happy and to be able to "fit" into the foreign culture. Children who are raised with a healthy attitude to both cultures and learn to appreciate cultural diversity will not have major problems making friends and fitting in. However, there is no doubt that they tend toward those who speak their home language. My girls love to be with their English-speaking friends.'

(Margo Arango, Colombia)

'Share your culture with your children's school by teaching a lesson about the culture, traditions, and share some food. The children come to respect and understand others. When children start school they are influenced by the school culture a great deal. As a parent you must be a part of that culture to have an influence. We expose our children to a wide variety of cultures, languages through fairs, friends, and travelling. Teach your children about both cultures and languages. Take them to visit their relatives back home. Let them know how important it is to you. Tell them stories about when you were young.'

(Mother in North Carolina)

'I think the children have to be placed in situations where they have no choice but to communicate in the minority language.'

(Sean Golden, Barcelona)

'Try to balance the exposures to the languages the children are learning. The less balanced the languages are outside the home, the more the home environment needs to counter the imbalance by concentrating on the less frequently used language. Don't switch back and forth. If presented with language mixing in a conversation, or worse yet, in individual utterances (we've seen this), children will pick one language and stick with it. Expose them maximally to both, at all levels. The ideal is to be able to have parallel tracks, so that everything experienced in one language and culture is also experienced in the other. This is obviously impossible for all situations, but the closer you can come, the better.'

(Charles Hoequist, USA)

'I used to recite nursery rhymes and fairy tales to the children, in English, when they were young. My sister sent me some tape recordings of children's songs, sung in English, that I played as background music while the children were playing. They mimicked the songs, which meant they were acquiring English phonemes. I think that this kind of "passive" reinforcement can be very useful. It was just there in the background with no coercion or demand that they do anything about it. I did the same with Irish songs and they also mimicked the Irish.'

(Sean Golden, Barcelona)

' • Total consistency in all situations (one can always explain and translate).

• Insistence that the child uses the minority language; this creates a need similar to not being understood, and removes any choice, as is normal in monolingual acquisition anyway.

• Creating a rich language environment through play, books, videos, songs, as many other interactants as possible (but that is often hard to achieve).

• Being positive about the linguistic progress the child makes (however minimal), and giving the child a positive feeling about her bilinguality (treats that only happen to children who speak German because they are part of the German culture, positive arguments for being bilingual "what is better, one piece of chocolate or two?", modelling reactions to negative feedback from peers when the situation occurs).'

(Susanne Döpke, Australia)

Conclusion

Some parents choose not to speak their language to their children for various reasons. Others make an attempt to use their language with their children, but abandon the venture after a period due to various pressures from the children, their partner or the world outside the family or never really get started. Nonetheless, children in every country are growing up with two languages which are not both spoken by their peers. They have vastly different family situations and the languages involved include most of the languages of the world. When they become adults, some of these children will be indistinguishable from their monolingual peers in both languages; others will have less than native mastery of one of the languages.

All in all, the matter of whether and how children are to be given the gift of two languages must be left in the hands of their parents. While bringing up a child with two languages is not difficult, it requires commitment and perseverance on the part of both parents. There is, as we have shown in this book, a good deal you can do to support your child's development in both their languages. The single most important factor in how successful you and they will be in this respect is, however, your and their *motivation*.

Good luck!

Organising a workshop on raising children with two languages

The workshop has three primary aims:

1   to gather those parents, teachers and others in the local community who are concerned with children growing up with two languages in the hope that they will get to know each other for a mutual exchange of experiences and tips
2   to establish contact with those who represent the local authorities and schools in questions concerning the position of pupils who have home languages and who may require support in the majority language
3   to develop ideas together to support children's development in both languages and possibly to make the initial contacts necessary to start minority language groups where children can meet others with the same minority language and develop their language (for example, toddlers' group, play-group or Saturday school).

The workshop is designed to fit into an evening, with the option of getting together for a follow-up evening if there is enough interest. A possible arrangement is the following:

| 7:00 | People arrive, register (so they can be informed about further meetings and groups which are set up), choose a topic of interest for | Have a number of pages prepared with room for eight to ten names on each. The papers should be labelled with a topic, for example, How can we optimise our children's linguistic development? How can we help our children to appreciate both their cultures? How can immigrant parents improve their knowledge of the majority language? How can we get |

	group discussion, pay the admission fee if there is one, and settle down.	the most out of our family's stay in this country? How can we support our children's schoolwork in the majority language if we don't speak it well? How can we make the most of an intercultural and/or mixed language marriage? Select topics on whatever suits the participants' interests. As people arrive have them choose which subject they want to discuss and write their name on one of the papers. Anybody wanting to be in the same group as a friend should write their name on the same piece of paper. Give each participant a name tag they can write their name on and pin/stick on their chest. They can also indicate on their name tag whether they are a parent, teacher or whatever.
7:15	Introduction and keynote speaker, with questions from the floor.	Your speaker should be someone who can speak knowledgeably about bilingualism, intercultural relationships, children's language acquisition and/or second language learning.
8:00	Getting into groups, according to the chosen topic.	Each group has a leader assigned by the organiser. If possible, refreshments can be served while the participants are getting into their groups, so they can take their cup with them to the group.
8:15	Groups discuss their topics. They can also brainstorm for ideas about their topic.	Problems associated with the topics are taken up and maybe solutions are offered and experiences shared. The leaders are well prepared with questions and try to keep in the background of the discussion as much as possible. They should make sure everybody gets a say. The leaders take notes and/or make a mind-map of any brainstorming activities. If all or some of the group want to meet again to set up a regular activity, for example, a Spanish language play-group, a French-speaking fathers' club or whatever, this can be arranged. A

9:00	All participants reassemble.	contact person should be nominated, so other participants can get in touch. Leaders report on each group's discussion, giving information about any follow-up activities the group participants want to plan.
9:30 onwards	Panel debate with keynote speaker, representative of the establishment and a couple of well-prepared parents.	The subject of the debate could be 'Growing up here with two languages'. Let each participant speak uninterrupted for, say, five minutes and then answer each other. Open the discussion to the floor when it seems appropriate. The discussion can then go on until all participants have said what they have on their minds.
End		The organiser might want to round off with a few words, and maybe suggest having another workshop in the future.

The person organising the workshop needs to work out the following details:

- Think of people you would like to have come and speak at the workshop and make arrangements with them. You need a keynote speaker (maybe a researcher or teacher) and someone who can give a completely different kind of perspective for the final debate, maybe a local politician. Decide on your date with your speakers.
- Find a suitable location. While it is very difficult to estimate how many will come, try to find somewhere where everybody can sit together and listen to a speaker and then break up into groups for discussion and coffee.
- If you have to pay for the use of the room, or for speakers, you will have to charge admission. Make sure you don't leave yourself out of pocket. There may be money available from some authority or other for this kind of activity.
- Recruit and prepare your leaders for the evening. Apart from being generally helpful, collecting admission fees, giving out name tags, serving coffee, etc., they will need to lead the group discussion and be prepared to report on it so all participants are informed about what all groups have discussed.

- Arrange tea or coffee and biscuits or whatever refreshments are appropriate in your country. You'll also need name tags, pens, paper and an overhead projector and maybe a tape recorder for your speakers if these things are not already in the room.

Ways to support a child's development in two languages

Parent and children group

The aim of this kind of group is to let minority language parents and pre-school children meet other children and parents with the same minority language to sing and play. Most groups meet once a week for about two hours, but other arrangements are possible. If there is a large minority language community, you may be able to meet more often. Not everyone can come every time.

What do you need?

The first priority is to investigate the matter of funding. There may be money and/or other help available from municipal authorities for this kind of group. Maybe you can also get help from the authorities to find somewhere to have the group's meetings. Otherwise, finding a suitable location is the next problem. You will need either to borrow toys that are already there or to buy your own toys and store them in the room you use. Village halls and churches may have their own play-groups or play areas. Perhaps you can use such a room and borrow the toys without having to pay too much (or even for free). You will need access to toilets and changing facilities.

It can sometimes be difficult to get a group of parents and children together. Some tips for getting to know others with the same minority language are given under Networking in Chapter 6 'Practical parenting in a bilingual home'. A workshop of the kind described in Appendix A can be a good way to meet others in the same situation as you. You might consider advertising your play-group, either in local shops, religious meeting places, childcare centres, clinics, etc., or in a local newspaper.

You may want to have some kind of snack during the group's meeting. Parents can take it in turn to bring something along if that is what works best. You could have a duty roster where parents can sign up for particular weeks. They can then be responsible for arriving early and getting things ready, staying behind to clear up after the meeting is over as well as providing the snack. If the group is big, maybe two parents will be needed each time. The parent whose turn it is can also lead the group if any leadership seems necessary, although groups often work out a more or less set order of events. Some activities will need preparation.

Younger pre-school children are not always open to too much organising and may prefer just to play with the toys. If the parents get involved with their play they can make sure there is plenty of language happening. Songs, finger play and a simple story are often all the structured activity the under-3s can deal with. Arnberg (1987) gives an example of a possible order of events in this kind of play-group, involving planned free play with dolls or cars, active play with singing games, talking about a topic with pictures, snack, song and finger games, drawing or clay and a story, with each activity being allotted 15 to 20 minutes. Many of the activities might be beyond the youngest children. This is not a problem, since the parents are available to activate them in some other way. Perhaps the younger ones can play some more with the toys while the older children draw.

Things to bear in mind:

- There should probably be at least ten children in the group, to prevent it petering out too easily when somebody leaves or cannot come several times in a row.
- It is generally not a good idea to have a child come along with a majority language-speaking parent, unless they usually speak the minority language together. To avoid confusing things the group's meetings must be kept free of the majority language.
- The group is for the children's benefit, not primarily a chance for the parents to chat. Left to themselves children of this age are likely either to use the majority language or just to play quietly by themselves. The parents need to play and talk *with* the children to stimulate their use of the minority language.

Minority language play-school

The difference between the parent and children groups discussed above and this kind of group is that in a play-school setting the parents leave their children with a teacher or leader. For this reason, this kind of group is better suited to older pre-school children, around 3–6 years. In some countries children start school during this period, in which case another arrangement may be better. But assuming that a group of 3–6 year olds can be assembled, this can be a beneficial impetus to their use of the minority language. Of course, the success of this kind of arrangement lies almost entirely in the hands of the teacher. She (such teachers are usually women) will need to be very capable and inspire confidence in young children who do not know her and their parents. Many children, especially the younger ones, might refuse to be left. Many teachers are unwilling to have parents around, especially if only some of the children have their parents there. Nonetheless the children might need a settling-in period with a parent nearby, perhaps waiting in another room. Could the waiting parents arrange some amusement for themselves? What about playing Scrabble or doing crosswords together or having a reading circle to read books in the minority language and then discuss them? Such activities all play their part in keeping the parents' language skills fresh.

Depending on the size and age of the group, the teacher may need a helper. In some groups, parents take it in turns to help the teacher, but this does not always work out too well in our experience, and it might be better to employ an assistant teacher. This kind of group is generally more expensive for parents unless local authorities can subsidise it. The teacher and assistant will usually need to be paid, as well as any rental to be paid for the use of a room and the cost of toys, equipment and stationery. This kind of play-school is often one afternoon a week, but if the parents' budget can stretch to twice a week it is probably better from the children's point of view.

Checklist for play-school organisers

The person organising needs to take care of the following matters:

- Funding: balance the books! How much does rent, equipment and teachers' pay cost? Look into grants. How much should parents pay?
- Location: where can the play-school be (see above for suggestions)?
- Recruit a teacher. She needs to be a native speaker of the minority language, but she should be aware of the majority culture that most of the children have lived in all their lives. We once had a newly arrived American teacher in an English play-school in Sweden who

tried to talk to the children about *Star Trek*, which had not been shown in their lifetimes on Swedish TV.

- Get together a group of children. There should probably be at least 12 children in the group. Any monolingual minority language children are a great asset in the group to help prevent the other children slipping into the majority language.

Saturday school

Once children reach school age they do not have much spare time. They may have a series of activities ranging from football to ballet to chess, as well as all the time they spend with friends, playing computer games, and maybe even doing homework. An extra morning or afternoon at school might not stand very high on their list of things to do! Nonetheless, if the minority language community is large enough, it might be possible to get together a group of children to study the minority language. Many countries offer no provision for home language teaching of children who have a minority language at home, leaving it up to the parents whether their children become literate in the home language or not. Parents might find it easier to support their children's literacy in the minority language together with other children.

Ideally, a qualified teacher should be enlisted to help, but if that is not possible, perhaps the parents can pool their resources. The parents need to get together and work out what they want from the Saturday school (which can equally well happen on another day), i.e. whether the children are aiming at going back to school in the home country or if it is enough for them to attain reasonable reading fluency to open the world of children's literature in the minority language. Are the children to learn to write and spell in the minority language? There are materials and support available from home-schooling organisations and groups here and there. Otherwise, parents might contact schools and teachers in the home country for advice about materials and methods.

The practicalities of setting up a Saturday school are not any different from those for the other groups: funding should be looked into, but may not be available. A room needs to be found, though toys are not necessary. If there are only a few children involved they might be able to meet at each other's homes. A teacher must be recruited if the parents are not to do the teaching. Books and writing materials need to be bought.

Children of school age are capable of making their own decisions about many things. Parents may need to put some work into motivating their children to want to go to school in their free time. However much fun you try to make it, reading and writing are very like what the children do all week at school. If they are not motivated, they will not enjoy their Saturday school, and are unlikely to learn very much.

Good luck in anything you organise for your children!

Appendix C

Documenting a child's linguistic development

The sheets in this appendix are intended for you to use to keep track of your child's acquisition of languages. Copy the sheets with a photocopier or by hand with a pencil and ruler. You might prefer to make your own sheets on a computer using a word processor (for example Microsoft Word™) or a calculation program (for example Microsoft Excel™). Have a file or notebook especially for your notes about your child's languages. You can record anything else you notice about your child's linguistic progress. You can use these sheets to see if one language is maybe slipping behind the other. This may be known and expected, but the sheets give a measure of what is going on and a chance to see if anything the family changes has an effect on the relative strengths of the child's languages.

Vocabulary

There are several ways you could keep track of your child's acquisition of languages. One way is to test vocabulary at different stages. Sheet 1 can be used to compare the child's vocabulary in both languages. You can start by writing the child's *first* 50 words in each language, and letting the next test be six months later. For children up to 3 or 4 you can use a picture book of the kind that has pictures of maybe 100 everyday objects without any text. The idea is that each parent (or other person the child uses each of the two languages with) sits in turn with the child and goes through the book talking about the pictures, seeing which objects the child can name.

For older children you can find a picture book of the kind that has very detailed pictures with lots going on, ideally so that there is no text visible on the page, or cards that show pictures of familiar objects. The level of difficulty can be increased as the child's language develops. Have a range of material each time, so there are always *some* words the child knows in both languages. Make the test into a game, and give children only positive feedback, concentrating on what they know rather than what they do not know. Use the test as a chance to teach new vocabulary and talk about new words. If you repeat the test in each language after six months you might see that the child's vocabulary has increased.

Length of utterance

You may also want some way of documenting and comparing the child's progress in learning to put words together in each language. Crystal (1986: 139–141) suggests measuring a child's mean length of utterance (MLU), which is a measure often used in child language research where concepts such as 'the two word stage of language development' (when a child typically uses two word sentences such as 'Mummy come') have been found useful. Sheet 2 is intended to be used in conjunction with tape recordings of the child's speech in each language, about 15 chatty minutes in each language. On Sheet 2 you can write out 100 consecutive sentences from the child's speech in each language, such as 'mine!', 'more milk' or 'I don't want to go to school'. If you have difficulty deciding where a particular utterance ends, leave that one out. You can count the total number of words in the 100 sentences then divide by 100 which gives the mean length of utterance. The above utterances have one, two and seven words, respectively. Up to a certain age you can follow your child's mean length of utterance as it increases in each language. The assumption is that longer utterances are a sign of more complex sentence structures, but after a certain level is reached the measure does not reflect language development, since sentences can become more complex without getting longer and vice versa.

Language mixing

Interference between your child's languages is interesting to observe, but you may wish to try to minimise it. It is a good idea to see first how much the languages affect each other, and later see if anything you are doing is helping to reduce the mixing. You can use Sheet 2 for this test too, but as well as counting words in each utterance, you can count instances where the child uses a word from the 'wrong' language. An utterance like 'more mjölk' instead of 'more milk' or 'mera mjölk' would, for example, be counted as having 50 per cent mixing whether it was 'supposed' to be

English or Swedish. If you count the total number of words in each utterance and the number of words from the other language you can add them up at the end and get an average for the hundred utterances.

Pronunciation

All children have difficulties with the pronunciation of some of the sounds of a language. Some sounds are simply harder to make than others, such as words where two or more consonants come together at the beginning and/ or end of the word, for example, *blanket, stop, crunched*. Other sounds are difficult in themselves, such as the <th> sounds in *think* or *the*.

Sheet 3 is meant for you to 'mark' your child's pronunciation. The idea is that you listen out for problems in your child's speech. Some of the problems will be of the kind that a monolingual child might have, while others will clearly be a kind of foreign accent. You can use any of the material you have recorded, but if you want to get children to try to say a certain sound you can ask them to read a simple sentence with the sound in or show them a picture of an object whose name contains the sound, or you can say sentences to them and have them repeat after you. It can be very difficult to spot children's pronunciation difficulties when you are speaking to them, but if you listen to their speech on a tape you might notice all kinds of things. You may wish to help your children practise special sounds if they have difficulty with them.

Children with two languages may sometimes speak their minority language with an accent like speakers of the majority language have when they speak the minority language. This probably means that the child is using some of the nearest sounds of the majority language instead of minority language sounds and may be following the phonological rules of the majority language in other ways too, so that a Spanish–French-speaking child in Spain may have difficulty pronouncing a French word which begins with <sp>, for example, *sport* is pronounced *esport* or a Swedish–English-speaking child in Sweden may be reluctant to pronounce the final sound in words like *was* as /z/ rather than as /s/.

The point of keeping track is to spot any problems and to see how children progress through the sounds and sound combinations of their languages. In Sheet 3 you can write the word the child is aiming at and describe what the child is doing wrong. Next time round, say after six months, you can try the problem words again. If the child's pronunciation has improved you may discover new problems which were not noticeable before.

Sheet 1 Vocabulary development

Date: _____   Age: _____

	Object	Language 1	Language 2	Comments
1				
2				
3				
4				
5				
6				
7				
8				
9				
10				
11				
12				
13				
14				
15				
16				
17				
18				
19				
20				
21				
22				
23				

24			
25			
26			
27			
28			
29			
30			
31			
32			
33			
34			
35			
36			
37			
38			
39			
40			
41			
42			
43			
44			
45			
46			
47			
48			
49			
50			

Sheet 2 Mean length of utterance and language mixing

Date: _____   Age: _____   Language _____

	Sentence	No. words	No. mix
1			
2			
3			
4			
5			
6			
7			
8			
9			
10			
11			
12			
13			
14			
15			
16			
17			
18			
19			
20			
21			
22			
23			

24			
25			
26			
27			
28			
29			
30			
31			
32			
33			
34			
35			
36			
37			
38			
39			
40			
41			
42			
43			
44			
45			
46			
47			
48			
49			
50			

51			
52			
53			
54			
55			
56			
57			
58			
59			
60			
61			
62			
63			
64			
65			
66			
67			
68			
69			
70			
71			
72			
73			
74			
75			
76			
77			

78			
79			
80			
81			
82			
83			
84			
85			
86			
87			
88			
89			
90			
91			
92			
93			
94			
95			
96			
97			
98			
99			
100			

Total no. words ___ /100 = MLU ___ No. mixed words ___ *100/total no. words = % mixing ___

Sheet 3 Pronunciation

Date: _____   Age: _____   Language: _____

	Word	Problem
1		
2		
3		
4		
5		
6		
7		
8		
9		
10		
11		
12		
13		
14		
15		
16		
17		
18		
19		
20		
21		
22		
23		
24		
25		
26		
27		
28		
29		
30		

Appendix D

Internet resources

Web sites

Bilingual Families Web Page

http://www.nethelp.no/cindy/biling-fam.html

This is a very useful starting point with information about raising children with two languages and plenty of links to other resources. It will show you the way to books, tapes, videos and software in, for example, Arabic, Chinese, Dutch, English, French, German, Hungarian, Italian, Japanese, Korean, Nordic languages, Spanish and Portuguese. The site discusses myths about bilingualism, discusses the politics of bilingualism and offers practical tips to visitors.

International Couples Homepage

http://www.geocities.com/Heartland/4448/Couples.html

This is a site for couples of different nationalities where you can find other mixed nationality couples. There is a list where couples can give information about themselves and invite other couples to contact them to exchange experiences.

Bilingual Parenting in a Foreign Language

http://www.byu.edu/~bilingua/

The goal of this page is to focus on families where neither parent is a native speaker of the target language and at least one parent is speaking that language (the target language) to the child(ren). The site also has an extensive list of resources and references which should be useful to any parents raising their child(ren) bilingually.

Meeting places

Biling-Fam Internet mailing list

This is a good place to exchange tips with others who are raising children in a variety of languages. It is run by Cindy Kandolf, an American living in Norway. You can choose how you want to receive the messages – one by one as they come in or in a digest version with several messages in a single email every few days. To subscribe to the mailing list send an email to

biling-fam-subscribe@nethelp.no

If you want the digest version, send the email to

biling-fam-digest-subscribe@nethelp.no

The Foreign Wives Club

http://www.foreignwivesclub.com/

The Foreign Wives Club is an online community designed to offer information, resources and support to women in bicultural marriages around the world. They have an online message board and articles and other material of interest to families living with two languages.

Multilingual Munchkins

http://www.multilingualmunchkins.com/

This is a site which also has an associated mailing list. Go to http://groups.yahoo.com/group/multilingualmunchkin/ for joining information.

ParentsPlace

http://www.parentsplace.com/

This is a parenting web site which has a board for discussing children with two languages. The ParentsPlace 'Bi–Lingual Children' chatboard had many relevant topics of discussion when we visited it.

http://pages.ivillage.com/robinshe/bilingual/ is the web page associated with the ParentsPlace message board.

Kids Bilingual Network

http://hjem.wanadoo.dk/~wan42942/frameset.html

This provides contact information to help parents of bilingual or multilingual children get in touch with others in similar situations.

Locating material

There is a problem in certain countries with using video tapes which were bought in another country, because there are several different standards in use. The NTSC standard for television transmission and video recording is used in Japan and North America; France uses SECAM; the rest of Europe, Australia and New Zealand use PAL. Other countries will use one or other of these standards. People in Sweden, for example, have no difficulty viewing videos bought in the UK, but US videos must be converted or viewed on a special multistandard machine.

Infanaj Kantoj

http://southern.edu/~caviness/kantoj.html

Children's songs and rhymes in German, English, French, Russian, Portuguese, Swedish and Welsh can be found here. Some of the songs have attached midi (music) files so you can hear the tunes.

6000 Volkslieder, German and other Folksongs, Genealogy, Ahnenforschung, Folksongs, Gospel

http://ingeb.org/

This German site has songs, many with music files, from 32 countries.

Bilingual/ESL Resources

http://www-bcf.usc.edu/~cmmr/BEResources.html

The Center for Multilingual, Multicultural Research at the University of Southern California provides a very extensive list of resources. It is intended primarily for teachers of English as a second language but there are also useful resources for parents.

Internet bookshops

There are many Internet bookshops available. Most of them serve the English-speaking market, but there are many others. These bookshops are generally happy to accept orders from other countries and have a fixed scale of postage charges. You pay by credit card and your books arrive after a few days.

- We have used the British W.H. Smith site extensively without difficulty as a good source of British books (http://www.bookshop.co.uk). They have no problem with posting books to Sweden. If you live in the European Union you may have to pay duty on books sent from outside the EU.
- Amazon is one of the biggest Internet bookshops, with sites in the UK (http://www.amazon.co.uk), Germany (http://www.amazon.de), as well as in the USA (http://www.amazon.com).
- For other bookshops with material in other languages, consult a web search tool, for example, your country's local version of the web catalogue Yahoo! (http://www.yahoo.com). There is a country-by-country resource list in the Bilingual Family page.
- World of Reading is a US-based company specialising in books, audio tapes and NTSC video tapes and software in a variety of languages (http://www.wor.com/). It will post material to other countries.
- Books Without Borders has children's books, videos and audio cassettes in English, Spanish, Russian, German, French and Italian (http://www.bookswithoutborders.com/). It also has some bilingual (English–French and English–Spanish) books for children.

Glossary

Dominant language   the language in which an individual is most proficient

First language   the language or languages an individual acquires as an infant

Foreign language   a language learned in a classroom setting – not the majority language

Fossilisation   when a second language learner no longer improves his or her imperfect mastery of the language

Interference   the effect that one of the languages spoken by an individual has on another

L1   first language

L2   second language

Language acquisition   gaining proficiency in a language in a setting where the language is spoken naturally

Language learning   gaining proficiency in a language in a classroom-like setting

Language mixing   using words from more than one language in a single utterance

Language switching   changing from one language to another

Majority language   the language spoken by most of the people in a country or region, often as their only language

Minority language   a language spoken by a small group of people (e.g. a family or an immigrant community)

Native speaker   an individual who has the language as his or her first (and often only) language

Near-native or native-like speaker   an individual who masters a language so well that native speakers cannot detect any foreignness

One language–one location   a system of using languages within a family so that each language is associated with a place rather than a person. The usual arrangement in this system is that the minority language is spoken at home and the majority language is spoken outside the home

One person–one language   a system of using languages within a family and elsewhere so that any two people always use the same language when speaking together

Second language   a language acquired later than the first language(s) in a setting where the language is spoken naturally

Bibliography

Arnberg, L. (1987) *Raising Children Bilingually: The Pre-school Years*. Clevedon, UK: Multilingual Matters.

Baker, C. (1995) *A Parents' and Teachers' Guide to Bilingualism*. Clevedon, UK: Multilingual Matters.

Bannert, R. (1984) Problems in learning Swedish pronunciation and in understanding foreign accent. *Folia Linguistica* 18: 193–222.

Bannert, R. (1984) Prosody and intelligibility of Swedish spoken with a foreign accent. In C.-C. Elert, I. Johansson and E. Strangert (eds) Nordic Prosody III. Papers from a Symposium. *Acta Univ. Umensis. Umeå Studies in the Humanities* 59: 7–18.

Crystal, D. (1986) *Listen to your Child*. Harmondsworth: Penguin.

Cunningham-Andersson, U. (1995) Native and non-native perception of dialectal variation in Swedish. In K. Elenius and P. Branderud (eds) Proceedings of the XIIIth International Congress of Phonetic Sciences, vol. 1: 278–281.

Cunningham-Andersson, U. and Engstrand, O. (1988) Attitudes to immigrant Swedish – a literature review and preparatory experiments. *Phonetic Experimental Research, Institute of Linguistics, University of Stockholm (PERILUS)* 8: 103–152.

Cunningham-Andersson, U. and Engstrand, O. (1989) Perceived strength and identity of foreign accent in Swedish. *Phonetica* 46(4): 138–154.

Cunningham, U. (2003) Temporal indicators of language dominance in bilingual children. In Proceedings from Fonetik 2003, *Phonum* 9, 77–80, Umeå University.

Doman, G. (1975) *How to Teach your Baby to Read*. Garden City, NY: Doubleday.

Döpke, S. (1992) *One Parent, One Language: An Interactional Approach*. Amsterdam: John Benjamins.

Flege, J. E. (1987) A critical period for learning to pronounce foreign languages. *Applied Linguistics* 8(2): 162–177.

Flege, J. E. (1993) Acquisition of prosody in a second language. Grant application to the Public Health Service. Manuscript, Dept of Biocommunication,

University of Birmingham, Alabama.

Foster-Cohen, S. H. (1999) *An Introduction to Child Language Development*, London and New York, Longmans.

Hanks, P. (ed.) (1986) *Collins Dictionary of the English Language*, 2nd edn. London: Collins.

Hansegård, N. E. (1975) Tvåspråkighet eller halvspråkighet? *Invandrare och Minoriteter* 3: 7–13.

Kotsinas, U.-B. (1994) The Stockholm dialect and language change. In G. Melchers and N.-L. Johannesson (eds), *Nonstandard Varieties of Language* (Acta Universitatis Stockholmiensis. Stockholm Studies in English 84). Stockholm: Almqvist and Wiksell.

Lambert, W. E. (1975) Culture and language as factors in learning and education. In A. Wolfgang (ed.), *Education of Immigrant Students*. Toronto: Ontario Institute for Studies in Education.

Lenneberg, E. H. (1967) *The Biological Foundations of Language*. New York: Wiley.

Major, R. (1990) L2 acquisition, L1 loss, and the critical period hypothesis. In J. Leather and A. James (eds), *New Sounds 90, Proceedings of the 1990 Amsterdam Symposium on the Acquisition of Second Language Speech*, University of Amsterdam, 9–12 April.

McAllister, R. (1990) Perceptual foreign accent: L2 users' comprehension ability. In J. Leather and A. James (eds), *New Sounds 90, Proceedings of the 1990 Amsterdam Symposium on the Acquisition of Second Language Speech*, University of Amsterdam, 9–12 April.

Penfield, W. (1965) Conditioning of the uncommitted cortex for language learning. *Brain* 88: 787–798.

Romaine, S. (1995) *Bilingualism*, 2nd edn. Oxford: Blackwell.

Saunders, G. (1982) *Bilingual Children: Guidance for the Family*. Clevedon, UK: Multilingual Matters.

Saunders, G. (1984) An interview with a Turkish–English bilingual. *Bilingual Family Newsletter* 1(2): 3.

Saunders, G. (1988) *Bilingual Children: From Birth to Teens*. Clevedon, UK: Multilingual Matters.

Scovel, T. (1988) *A Time to Speak: A Psycholinguistic Inquiry into the Critical Period for Human Speech*. New York: Newbury House/Harper and Row.

Skutnabb-Kangas, T. (1981) *Tvåspråkighet*. Lund: Liber Läromedel.

Swain, M. and Lapkin, S. (1982) *Evaluating Bilingual Education: A Canadian Case Study*. Clevedon, UK: Multilingual Matters.

Young, P. and Tyre, C. (1985) *Teach your Child to Read*. London: Fontana.

Index

Page numbers in **bold** type represent main entries